Sex, Drugs, and Yoga

Enjoy my story

♡

Birdie

Scan the QR code below
or search for Birdie Paradise's
Sex, Drugs, and Yoga playlist on Spotify
for a musical accompaniment to this book

Sex, Drugs, and Yoga

Birdie Paradise

First published in 2022
by Lemon Quartz Publishing Ltd
85 Great Portland Street, First Floor
London W1W 7LT
United Kingdom

001

The events depicted within this work have been recollected to the best
of the author's ability. Certain names and characteristics of people and
locations have been changed to maintain their anonymity.

Printed and bound in Great Britain by Clays Ltd, Elcograf S.p.A.

A CIP catalogue record for this book
is available from the British Library

ISBN: 978-1-7399076-0-0

To Brenna and Lana,
who remove the fatal from femme fatale.
Replacing it with alive.

In your late twenties, you mark a milestone known as the Saturn Return. Astrological adulthood. It takes this giant planet about twenty-nine years to complete one orbit around the Sun, at which point it returns to the exact position it held in the sky at the moment of your birth. It is a rite of passage.

29

|||| |||| |||| ||||

"Sex can cure loneliness."

January 7, 2004
Tuesday's gone.

I hooked up with three different guys this week. The list this month:

Chad
Kelsey
Paul
Rob
Kevin
Tom
Jonny
Reid
Brendan
Bryce

January 9, 2004
Last night I drank poison at a party. Someone got it on film. Me pouring a shot of Lysol into my mouth. In the video, my head comes forward, and a bubble emerges out of my throat and into the air.

If it had been a more significant quantity, say even a few gulps, according to the label, I would be dead.

Last night I had a taste of death.

January 12, 2004

I suffer with anxiety. At times it's quite intense. I hate how it feels, and I want to escape it. How do you break free from a feeling that lives inside yourself? Apparently it's a fairly common thing. Anxiety. Something that percentages of people are inflicted with all over the world. Is that supposed to offer some sort of comfort? That others are also plagued with feeling this way? I'm not sure. It's also a taboo. None of us can talk about it.

Today's attack started at the community pool because I can't believe how fat I look in a bikini. I contemplated going home but my stuff was in Lana's locker, locked. Stuck to deal with myself in a bathing suit. To compensate, I make raunchy jokes. It is evident that overweight girls are not attractive enough to be silent. This makes me sad.

Sad, fat me.

February 9, 2004

The nice guys, the ones who talk to me, are asking about my preferences in terms of relationships. For me to like someone he mustn't have any need for me. This will pique my interest.

As evidence of this conundrum, there is Matt. A nice, smart, and funny guy. He's quirky. Then Bryce, who ignores me and makes me feel like shit. He's hot. All my girlfriends hate his guts.

I like Bryce.

March 13, 2004

Bryce has a series of female visitors. I don't know if any of them are his girlfriend. They probably all are. Bryce is the type to be with at least three people at all times.

At the strip club where I was watching women get naked for money, I started to have what felt like an intense breakdown. I needed someone to comfort me. I called Ashley's boyfriend as well as Bryce. Drunk, I can't remember what was said or who is to blame for how unreasonable the conversation was. What I know today is that Bryce hung up on me.

So I went home with Ashley's boyfriend instead.

Sex can cure loneliness. Having sex for this reason is OK if it isn't with your friend's boyfriend. Luckily, Ashley seems to understand that I didn't sleep with her boyfriend to hurt her, but because I hurt.

March 18, 2004

I've decided to replace Quirky Matt with Simon. He is awesome. A characteristic that I saw waning in Matt. Nice guys who I have caged in the friend zone will only be nice to someone like me for a limited amount of time. Then some kind of sexual frustration wins. Recently, this left me for a few days with no one to talk to. No one to cry on. No one to hang out with and make jokes to. Until I found Simon.

March 19, 2004

I tried one more time to see if Matt would hang out with me. Maybe my ditching of him was premature. Maybe his quirkiness is charming. It went well until he told me he heard something about anal sex. Something derogatory. Involving me.

I suspect he isn't congratulating me on being adventurous. On the contrary, this feels like the world's way of calling women sluts. Being called names hurts. To cry really loudly seems an appropriate response. Exasperated, I plan to sleep on the floor. Exactly where Matt left me.

March 20, 2004

I want to get out and smile as the sun shines onto my surroundings. I want to run. The rush I get from the movement

3

and air stops me from feeling sorry for myself. It's just me, footsteps, and sun-soaked leaves.

March 21, 2004

I am in New York for five days. By far the largest metropolis I have ever seen. Manhattan can hit like a wall. There are students here from all over the world. Like me, but nothing like me. The US Department of Homeland Security have presented a slideshow on terrorism. I look to the delegates in the front row, the ones from Egypt, and try to picture how embarrassed they must be. Because according to Homeland Security, Egyptians are terrorists. I want to cry again. This time for the hypocrisy of the world. Not just the slut-shaming. After the presentation, the American student beside me does not agree with how horrible this culture is. His blatant disregard makes me question life in general. The point of it. Maybe it's just a series of opportunistic interactions meant to fill the void of a transient existence of discontinuity and disillusionment. But maybe it is something else. Something more.

April 19, 2004

Last night I ate a large quantity of mushrooms. Of the psilocybin, not porcini, variety. To some people, taking hallucinogens the night before final exams is a bad idea. I am not one of those people.

Mushrooms give me a feeling of grandeur, an omnipresent existence. This feeling is mixed with vivid, kaleidoscopic scenes. Spinning rainbows, dripping colours, and liquid-filled tubes – all surging. The visions have a rhythmic quality. They give me energy. Everything emanates from within.

I called a cab to take me home from my friend's place. The cab was a flying, glass-domed capsule. It drove me through a galaxy of laser lights and starbursts. Nowhere to be seen were the simple roadside sights of London plane trees, a strip mall boasting Home Depot or Fairway groceries, or any other mundane side streets off Mackenzie Ave in Saanich, Victoria.

In my bed, the sheets feel like butter satin. Tiny butter satin snakes engulf my skin. I tremble as the mushrooms bubble in my stomach. My room and its contents grow to an exaggerated jungle of enormous proportions. Cartoon jaguars and vines fill the room from floor to ceiling. I get out of bed and try to capture the felines and cut the vines.

I wake up realizing that I've made quite the mess.

There's broken glass, evidence of a fire in the garbage can, and about ten pairs of shoes thrown out the window. I return from the grass below with the better half of my shoe collection. Mostly newly purchased in New York.

Matt doesn't find taking hallucinogens funny. Instead, he calls me irresponsible. Like a thirteen-year-old. My standard behaviour. He says.

May 10, 2004

I've been smoking a lot of weed. People confront me about what I want in life. Instead of giving an honest answer, my response is a ramble. One meant to amuse.

In conclusion: I want to have sex.

This seems crass to admit. But it's the truth. Based on my reply, people deduce that I am easily bored. This is why I remain unsatisfied. I deny this of course. Negating a theory fails to acknowledge the truth behind it. I am bored. But my attention span and appetite for stimulation is not something I feel like getting into during public conversation.

Another question comes up. The question about why I avoid looking people in the eyes.

Geoff asked me this today. Why I don't look him in the eyes. I respond that I don't know why. I say this staring at the wall, the ceiling, his ear.

The truth is I lack self-confidence.

Something about the eyes is too revealing. Looking into someone's eyes gives them the opportunity to look into mine. I don't want Geoff, or anyone else, to catch a glimpse of something they do not deserve.

My mind is racing. Because I do want to Love. To know what it feels like. To feel Love for myself and for another individual. Reciprocated. Unfortunately an intense fear is holding me back. My mind has a catastrophic way of thinking. It tells me that there's no point in the illusion of true Love because what I think it is, it is not. This is why I do not look people in the eyes. Because it's not the right time. I am not ready.

May 12, 2004
I didn't allow myself to get close to Geoff. Today he told me how he can't be serious with someone who hasn't seen a movie called Casablanca. So we're breaking up. I can forget Geoff. This is the beauty of the one-week relationship. An amount of time that amounts to nothing. A mere blink. Feeling sad about it is a waste of emotion. I feel sad enough on my own.

*

May 24, 2004
On a magnificent beach along the Pacific Rim, with nineteen others students from university, I vacation. An attempt to vacate. Somewhere where beanstalk pine trees reach for the sky above and thundering waves crash against light grey

sand and driftwood below. My friend Brenna is lying by my side at the intersection of where waves meet shore. In gentle whitewash, the muted sun highlights her light brown hair a partial strawberry and golden blonde. Her hazel eyes reflect permanent sparkle. The water laps up to my pelvis and brings energy and life. Then it retreats and removes fear and frustration. In the distance, towards the break, wetsuit-clad ninjas ride sideways on their surf boards. Bryce is one of them. Still ignoring me.

I try not to think of Bryce. I am in disguise. A long strand of sea kelp wraps around my hips and head. This is a costume of the sea. I just ate a few mushrooms. Just a few this time. Brenna, beaming beside me, looks at me to say this is happiness.

I want to believe her.

May 25, 2004

I met three guys who live near the ocean on a short bus. Precisely half the size of a regular bus. The interior is fitted out with kitchenette and bunk beds. The exterior is hand painted with black burning skulls and racing stripes. Due to the decoration of their home, I call these guys Skull Bus. Today I kissed one of them. His name also happens to be Matt. Not to confuse him with Quirky Matt, I am going to call him Skull Bus Matt. He is a part-time dishwasher and surfer in Tofino.

My conversation with Brenna about happiness is weighing on me. She seems so sure. Whereas I am not. I envy this about Brenna. Something that sets her apart from everyone else I know is that, no matter what she does, she always radiates sureness and happiness. She is magnificent. So I believe her. This beach, in Tofino, is happiness. For a moment I actually feel it.

7

If it is possible to ride a strong wave of bliss, then I should stay in Tofino and turn the moment into more. I want to stay here but my parents will not be amused when I tell them that my life ambition, after university, is to live in a short bus down by the ocean, swathed in seaweed.

*

June 1, 2004

For the summer, along with two of my girlfriends, I have been presented with the largest ski resort in North America, which happens to be accessible by crossing the Georgia Strait by ferry then driving up the Sea to Sky Highway. My accommodation, Ashley's family's Creekside cabin. With five-bedrooms, forged post and beam accents, a river rock fireplace, and outdoor hot tub, this is a luxury chalet. Ski season ends to make way for the golf and mountain bike season. Since tourists still come here to visit I can find employment in a chain restaurant that specialises in cheap Italian food for families and a retail store founded by an American outdoorsman to sell clothing, sportswear and outdoor gear. While I find work painfully boring, life in Whistler has changed my perspective on other things.

I am in the forest where I belong. Everything that I thought to be a certainty has changed. Back to knowing nothing.

June 5, 2004

I bought a skateboard. It's bloody awesome.

June 7, 2004

I can't sleep because I am so stressed about going back to school to my final year.

June 10, 2004

I want to glide. I don't care if it's sideways, backwards, or upside down. I just want to glide.

My new skater friends include five guys who wear black clothes, black eyeliner, and have dyed black hair. I call these guys MFS, which is short for Made For Skating. Last night I drank wine coolers with MFS and discussed things. Including the concept of a pain-free life. Life without physical nor mental adversity.

A painless life should be a maxim. The life one wants to live. But to MFS it is the opposite. Something so overwhelmingly impossible that they would self-destruct. This led us to talk about fear and eternal loneliness. Introspective conversation with skinny men who wear make-up is attractive. So I kissed MFS Justin. In Whistler there is an endless list of boys to kiss.

French Eric
First-night Patrick
John
18-year-old at Savage
Brent
Geoff
MFS Justin
Skull Bus Matt

I am not good for any of these guys and they're not good for me. So we kiss. Nothing more and nothing less.

Just meaningless meanderings.

June 17, 2004

Doing cocaine with some guy at the restaurant, I feel invincible. Then, totally helpless. This extreme contrast is daunting. But I also like it.

June 19, 2004

The best way to stop doing drugs at work is to stop going to work.

To fill newfound time this summer unemployed, I plan to see my roommate Ashley's latest hook-up. He is an Australian called Aussie-Phil.

A competitive side of me wants to seduce him. My recent past regarding Ashley's boyfriends is already a delicate topic. But the truth is that I saw Aussie-Phil first.

I used to think that there were enough guys to go around for everyone. Then I changed my mind.

June 22, 2004

Adam, another Aussie, has to leave the country. He is my favourite for things like holding hands. His ambivalence and independent nature fit well with my current capacity for a non-relationship. I like that our worlds are separated by the entire world. A vast amount of distance is comforting. It means that nothing I say or do matters because the day he gets on a plane it's all over. I prefer this.

June 23, 2004

The best thing about Australians is how they smell like sunshine.

Following the scent of sun, it leads to the Australians of Whistler.

June 24, 2004

I am on a combination of cocaine, mushrooms, caffeine pills, alcohol and marijuana.

Bam.

June 25, 2004

Food sits in my stomach like a log. Needing it out of me, I make myself puke using the handle end of a toothbrush.

June 26, 2004

I am overwhelmed by the drugs around me. I want to see what's over the hill, around the corner, beyond the bend in the road, over the mountain, and past the horizon. I want to feel something other than how I feel. To make this journey as interesting as possible means I must champion the existence of drugs.

Some people do life in colour. I do mine in fluorescent.

June 28, 2004

I owe it to myself to walk out of these front doors, towards the forest, and scream.

July 1, 2004

Partially hidden amongst the shadows and bushes bordering the Whistler Village car park entrance, I lie atop soft soil and visit another dark garden. Loneliness. There are so many words but no one to hear them. I hide and listen to the empty voices passing by, celebrating in the distance. So much for my own time to be loud. These passersby sound like ghosts, and I'm a corpse. Rotting and unnoticed.

Overhead, a bird flies above in the black sky against clouds. She sings my song. To deaf mountains and earless trees.

My girlfriends are out partying in matching red bikinis, pageantry sashes, and Indian feather head dresses. I can't handle attention or people looking our way. With or without alcohol. I can't handle it.

Time to hitchhike home. My thumb presses out extending sign language to someone driving this road.

July 2, 2004

Aussie-Adam left for Perth. I didn't say goodbye. There is no such thing as a happy ending. Just an ending.

In his absence I feel a silence. He took part of me with him. The tequila I consume does not change this. It does not replenish what is missing.

July 4, 2004

I ran into Geoff in front of Savage Beagle nightclub. When he saw me he smiled. I did not smile back. I did not make eye contact. He is a bottomless ocean.

Window shut and curtain closed. The lapping sea cannot seep inside. Cutting someone off is a process. One I am becoming master at. After I build a wall, all that's left is a memory. I will hold onto it like a secret. Something intangible. Our past. Our former association. It is nothing more than a secret. One that I have the power to erase if and how I choose to do so.

To forget.

Except for that awkward smile, I forgot Geoff.

August 1, 2004

My propensity to feel empty has turned into a problem. One called bulimia. The feeling of emptying my stomach after an excessive feast is relieving. It momentarily fixes me.

August 2, 2004

Kissing:

Ryan

Jules

Aussie-Phil
Doug
Jay

Looking at these names, it's ironic that the occasion for real intimacy is seldom. My latest intrigue is a young man named Carly who lives far away in Kelowna. I think of him like I think of some sort of valuable metal deposit that has not yet been mined to production. An untapped resource. We met at Ben Lee skate park. He can skate.

Unfortunately, I spent time with his friend not him. Apparently Carly has a girlfriend.

Just before meeting Carly, after Aussie-Phil hopped in the shower with me, there was a breakdown in relations between Ashley and myself. Interestingly, this makes me feel guilty and sad followed immediately by angry and full of resentment. It occurs to me that maybe I keep stealing Ashley's boyfriends because I don't like her. I thought she was my best friend but my actions indicate otherwise. The consequence of this rift will be interesting. Considering we are roommates in her parent's cabin.

August 3, 2004
The "island" theory of existence states that no matter what conditions I exist in, I am meant to be an island. Alone and impenetrable.

One day I will find a way to connect my island to a mainland. One day.

August 4, 2004
I remind myself that sadness waxes and wanes like the moon. I remind myself that sadness is OK. It is other emotions like anger and frustration that are useless. We can control the latter. But the cycle of sadness I cannot control.

13

It invades my being and I must share the space.

Sadness has washed over me and I feel totally helpless.

August 5, 2004

In the tall green grass surrounding Rainbow Lake lie five girls. Including the glorious Brenna. She came to visit and the sadness went away. We drink wine mixed with an array of other liquids. We call it the razz-dazzle.

With liquor-bathed eyes, Brenna and I discuss frivolous topics such as releasing an album for the band we started an hour ago.

Hanging out with Brenna helps me relax. I call this situational satisfaction. It happens when we achieve satisfaction and are also content. For me this occurs typically when sobriety and self-awareness vanish. Leaving room for nothingness and everything.

August 7, 2004

Ashley and I will never be friends again.

August 9, 2004

Hand in hand, Brenna and I ascend the winding log stairs to the second-story kitchen. Here the French Canadian who has been staying in one of the spare bedrooms is eating a sausage.

Brenna asks if we can paint him. Together we craft a striped vest and bow tie on his bare chest.

Our fun is interrupted by the ridiculous rear attachment, obscene racing stripes, and do-it-yourself tinted windows of an Acura pulling into the driveway. The base thumps and Tupac Shakur bellows through the window. Three Asian guys and one skinny non-Asian guy walk inside the house. The non-Asian is Ashley's brother. He is a terrorist. He is who the Department of Homeland Security should be using on their slideshow. Not an Islamist Egyptian.

Brenna and I leave. After clubbing, we entertain ourselves and others as acrobatic statues set in the village square garden. Money starts to fill the cup we've placed in front of us. A policeman arrives. He says stop. Leave the village and go home. We run. Into the local Subway sandwich franchise store and ask for bin bags. Clad in black plastic togas, no one, especially not the police, can recognise us. I love wearing a good disguise.

August 10, 2004

Ashley's brother held Brenna and I hostage inside one of the cabin's bedrooms last night. He went on a rampage and threatened to hurt us. There was nothing we could do but call the police. The attending officer was the same guy who banned us from busking in the village square. Saying nothing about our panhandling, he arrested Ashley's brother.

At this point it makes sense that I vacate her family's cabin.

After retrieving the French Canadian's guitar from the ravine, collateral damage from the raid, Brenna has agreed to flee the premises with me. Thelma and Louise style. We're blowing this popsicle stand.

August 12, 2004

My friend Jay, a cab driver and luxury vehicle chauffeur, is en route for the pickup.

It makes me happy to leave the ski resort, summer's worth of kissing list, skateboarding, and potpourri of drugs that circulate around the Whistler village.

My heart is racing. Brenna just got a phone call. From Matt. Quirky Matt.

He is proposing that we join him on a road trip across the United States. Perhaps he doesn't despise me after all.

28

‖‖ ‖‖ ‖‖ ‖‖ |

"I just learned, the soft way,
that penises don't work in the cold."

August 13, 2004

Jay delivered me and Brenna to Vancouver and our new home, a maroon Dodge Caravan with a single sliding door. I take stock of Matt. Red hair that needs a trim, a slight beard, porcelain skin except for tanned shoulders and cheeks. His personality presents as equal parts hilarious and composed. His childhood friend Dave will share the driving. It all seems perfect. Perfection in this moment is singing along to an array of music we play on a CD player that has been wired to the vehicle's audio system. Beside me, inside a plastic package, is a set of rabbit ears and a fluffy tail. We drive along Highway 7 then exit into a suburb to pull up at a house. A petite redhead lady waits out front of a lawn in Coquitlam to join Team Roadtrip. I hop out and place the rabbit ears on her head. The fifth and final member of our van family has arrived. We call her Bunny.

Off the highway a sign advertises free kittens. I ask Matt if I can have one and he says yes. Her name is Vegas and I keep her in my purse. It is ever more likely Matt doesn't hate me after all. So why do I feel so challenged by him?

August 14, 2004

Recently, it turns out, I lost my ID. Crossing a border without valid identification is a problem. A problem made worse by

Brenna's purse, which is allegedly saturated with illicit marijuana residue. From an Internet café, I print my academic records as proof to suggest that I will return to Canada. My fourth year at the University of Victoria commences in September. It has been paid for after all. In the washroom sink, Brenna washes her purse with soap.

We present US customs with proof of registration for an upcoming fall semester along with a thoroughly washed satchel. They deem this satisfactory and the van cruises south into the State of Washington, United States of America.

August 16, 2004

I lie somewhere called Dead Man's Pass inside a sleeping bag laid out under a picnic table. My existence is somewhat immune to rows upon rows of giant rigs and endless highway. A beautiful sleep is in the air. Interestingly, in this backdrop, which would be perfect for a murderous horror movie, I am not scared. The open sky and a sweet slumber descend.

August 17, 2004

The road is flanked by a steady array of advertisements. Each looms above. Each to instill fear about some topic like terrorism or mosquitos or West Nile virus.

By Boise, Idaho, the girls and I pick up matching gym-class pinneys, ballet tutus, and baseball socks. We progress to a discount used-clothing store in Salt Lake City, Utah. Matt and Dave buy suits in shades of powder blue with three pieces including tight waistcoats and flared trousers. More costumes on the campaign of distraction.

Thumbing the circular racks of fur jackets, I decide that I miss being more than friends with Matt. Inside the van the rift between us is as big as the distance we travel.

Dressed like a circus and unafraid of these killer American mosquitos, we dance amongst them on giant rolling sand dunes.

August 19, 2004

Without psychedelics, a real electro-luminous nebula surrounds me. Las Vegas. It's hot. Even at 3 am.

The boxed wine we had in the van disappears rapidly, replaced with calls from Las Vegas Boulevard. I march towards the ruckus then stand directly in front of the fountain outside Caesar's Palace to watch a musical cascade of golden spray. The world is silent in the glimmering water. Brenna and Bunny are down the strip at a pirate ship outside Treasure Island. They whistle.

We dance, observe, and act merry, then retreat back to the van.

Even in just our bras and panties with the door slid wide open it's too hot to sleep. So we sing back to the pirates of Las Vegas.

August 20, 2004

As the sun rises the boys return. Their suits are dusted with dry brown earth. In tow is a random man they met at a soup kitchen. He introduces himself, with an indeterminate accent, and then produces some white powder from a magazine flap.

After a crisp one off the dash, we decide to upgrade from a parking lot to a motel that charges by the hour. I can't wait to shower in something more than a sink. With bronzer and mascara in hand, the warrior prepares for an evening at war. In bright turquoise patent leather pumps, I am a huntress. Vegas is my prey.

August 21, 2004

Las Vegas proves to be a lot of hype with little outcome. It is entirely possible to out-scandal these surroundings. They call it Sin City but the reality is that there is little creative allure. That's a shame. We did not gain entrance into a single nightclub. And even had to leave the cheapest casinos. This is the problem with not holding proper identification. We did make a cameo in a music video production and took great photos.

August 23, 2004

Unwrapping a pre-boiled egg, the smell indicates that parading around the USA on a meagre budget is losing appeal. I have been eating mayonnaise packets from Burger King on day-old discount sandwich bread. A can of aerosol cheese sits on the dashboard. This road trip is starting to lose its novelty.

August 24, 2004

By Orange County, the ocean breeze evaporates the disgusting feel of Death Valley. We park and descend to Laguna Beach. In white sand, Brenna and I huddle under a random Californian's T-shirt to smoke a doobie. In the distance, skim boarders float and pump into the waves. The fact that people smoke weed in LA is awesome. Local marijuana is available to buy at pharmacies in Hollywood. They call this prescription grade.

People in LA have to be high all the time to deal with the traffic and social obsession with celebrity.

We met some girls in a car beside ours. Another Canadian and a local half-Mexican surfer joined the party. On my head sits a white trucker hat with the word Destroyer written across the front. This is a present from our new friends.

Destroyer is slang for being wasted or amazing. I fit both categories.

August 26, 2004

We are finally heading home via San Francisco. A confined space with a problem like Matt has challenged my previous ability to mitigate tense situations. No sound effect, joke, or staring into the distance works.

Out of my comfort zone.

The problem is me.

August 27, 2004

This time the issue is that Matt called me a narcissist in front of everyone. Instead of shutting him down I can only put on sunglasses and try to shut myself down.

My mind begins racing uncontrollably. Although I deeply appreciate Matt, not just because he gave me a Red Bull tank top but because I really like him, he has no problem publicly criticizing me. It seems that when people are hurt they can't help but wish a little hurt back upon the world.

Matt doesn't know how much I already hurt deep inside. Emotions that prevent anyone from seeing the truth: that I cannot handle the big insults.

September 6, 2004

Passing through the Red Wood trail along the Northern Californian and Oregon coast, we soon arrive at the border. Canadian Customs is bewildered about how I crossed into the US without ID. They lecture me to not attempt this again.

*

September 8, 2004

Back at university, the living quarters are tight but beautiful. My room is the living room and the bedroom belongs to my roommate, Nicole. She appears even more brilliant than last year. An attribute that rubs people up the wrong way. They call her a snob. I disagree. She is the picture of someone in control. Someone with poise.

September 11, 2004

Nicole and I talk a lot. Including about my growing paranoia. Her rebuttal is that instead of enjoying a moment or an occurrence for what it is, university teaches us to think critically all the time. We are praised for our own critical thoughts and how they complement or contrast the thoughts of others. We are encouraged to share via papers and discussion groups. This leads to over-analyzing. She thinks this is normal. Not a life sentence. Change is possible.

She too wishes to be less aware. She wishes she could swim through life more on the surface.

For this reason, her deep understanding and good advice, I love Nicole.

September 12, 2004

My memories are a haze. My hangovers rampant. Last night, the girls and I set out to Red Jacket nightclub at 11 pm. Being inebriated beyond the capacity to walk, I was asked to leave. I didn't care. In my mind it was 2 am and I needed neither accurate time nor ability to stand. Vaguely, I recall falling up the stairs. The joint I smoked while being tossed out was the exact size of my middle finger. Both proudly waving goodbye.

Sunrise revealed my clothing abandoned. I'm donning a skirt made out of someone else's T-shirt. Tucked inside my bra is a number to some 'GUYS'. I call it. Brenna answers.

September 15, 2004

Erin, my girlfriend from uni, and I are driving from Victoria to Tofino. Not to surf in a town known for surfing but to behave in poor judgement.

Carly, the untapped resource, is coming to meet us. This time he is apparently single. Otherwise we just found a group of fifteen men here to celebrate bachelordom with an outrageous party. After brief introductions, one of them passed me a 60 oz. bottle of Crown Royal. Whisky. Precisely at the moment the sun decided to make an appearance.

After a few deep swigs of the amber liquid my pants are off and I'm sporting a football helmet with beer cans attached to the sides. It's a motherfucking drinking helmet.

Erin, too, is pants-less. She is wearing a G-string bikini. Neither her ass cheeks nor my beer helmet bother anyone. We are wholly accepted.

September 16, 2004

The best man, six foot two and 230 lbs, and Erin, 95 lbs, are passed out, face first in the sand. Midway between the ocean and the periphery of the campsite. This is when Carly decided to show up. Instead of paying me any attention, he immediately took off into the breaking waves. Competing with the ocean for a surfer's attention is precisely what the whisky in me wants to attempt. Unfortunately, the whisky forgot how illogical it is to attempt passionate sex with a man who just spent several hours in northern Canadian ocean water. I just learned, the soft way, that penises don't work in the cold. They call this shrinkage.

Since the night of crazy sex I had planned is not going to happen, I am stuck with no camping supplies, no sleeping bag, and no blanket. I lie on gravel, freezing.

Erin lies in an oversized men's sweat suit cuddling the best man. They are like a baby and mama koala. No one is cuddling me. I am like an abandoned piece of garbage.

October 5, 2004

Since it has potential to be a happy place for me, I'm going to hang out in Tofino more. Which means that I have to actually tackle what people do here and learn to surf. This involves swimming into menacing water, through and past breaking waves, to a point in the distance that is calm. Then, I must stare behind my shoulder to spot a wave and swim to meet it. A race. Just me and my flailing arms in an attempted union of woman, board and swelling ocean water. If all works out, I must pop myself to standing and ride the wave sideways towards the shore.

Trying to get to a point where I can catch a wave involves near-drowning. The surfboard can easily smack you in the head. Failing at this is total frustration. Surfing for me is coughing out salt water. Crying.

This, it seems, is quite difficult.

I don't tell anyone that water makes me nauseous. The ocean gets inside me and shakes things up. I lie in bed and dip and bob and feel the water taunting my being.

Seasick, I vomit.

October 8, 2004

Back on land, Skull Bus Matt and I are inside the staff housing of a restaurant he washes dishes at. It smells like garbage and urine. We are accompanied by some locals. One of them is severely mentally debilitated. Matt explains that this is because of excessive alcohol abuse. First as a fetus and now throughout adult life. Normally I would be disturbed by these surroundings.

Some sort of fluid is on this man's hands and he is so close beside me that now it's on me. I am someone who cannot stand if one single lock of my own hair is out of place. I disinfect my footwear with detergent and like things clean and spotless. Despite these preferences, I don't flinch. I do not recoil in horror. I look directly into this person's eyes. Reality is not always pretty. Continuing to look inside him, I see a human. I can forget the rancid smell and the indeterminate stain on my clothing. But I'll never forget that we're all human.

I want to share this emotion with Matt. But words can't express what I want to say. I hope for communication by means of osmosis. Things like harsh reality and love and warmth and compassion and skanky vomit are things that must be felt to be understood. There's no point in telling Matt how I feel. They call it 'feeling' because it is tactile. It happens inside. No two people can ever feel exactly the same. We can only agree on a generalisation. In general, since my surfing career is coming to an abrupt end, so shall my relationship with Skull Bus.

We say goodbye, in the form of a hug. Close to him I continue to say nothing. Hopefully the humanness in my own eyes shines through.

27

卌 卌 卌 卌 |

"Between who you are and who you have the potential to be seems to be where there is hope."

October 10, 2004
Some people disagree about the possibility to abandon conventional norms. But I believe that it's entirely possible to abandon a life of complication in pursuit of more simple truths.

October 11, 2004
My body, physically, feels strange. Like I'm tripping out. But I'm sober. My mind is far away. Miles away from the reality of where I actually am and what I actually do.

October 20, 2004
Shin deep and sinking in the battle of self-discovery versus the expectations of society, I pick up the phone and press the illuminated buttons on the clear green plastic VTech receiver. With the cordless to my ear, anxiety swells with each ring. A conversation is happening. Three minutes of it feels like three hours of enduring draconian torture.

It would help if my parents, who, technically, know me, would say something encouraging.

They do not.

My limbs stretch. They administer electric shocks. This is what talking to my parents feels like. Sometimes drops of water stream down my face. I am bound. Anger and frustration consume my being. I am misunderstood. It appears that parents are family. So why can't they accept a black sheep daughter? Instead, they force a white wool coat.

I wonder if I'm speaking in English. After a long pause my mom replies with a story about Brussels sprouts. A great bargain at the local farmer's market. She and Dad plan to make stew for dinner. She hangs up.

I'm coming to understand why people employ selective listening. It is a psychological form of protection. My mom finds what I say unacceptable. I can't imagine what she'd do to protect herself from the things I don't say.

In reassurance, I eat an entire box of cereal.

October 25, 2004

Evidently I am at a crossroad between choosing what I want for myself and what my parents want for me. Because I crave their approval, their support, their encouragement. So I decide not to move to Tofino. I will do something else. Though what that is remains unknown.

After the capacity to Love, it seems the next best thing a human can do is to discover.

To discover is to find the truth. A quest that inspires me to go on. To continue. Otherwise, life doesn't seem worth living. My lows feel like they're getting lower.

October 26, 2004

I want to avoid the pain of a meaningless existence. Thinking I have a purpose is painful enough. A lot of my friends don't want to talk about this sort of thing. I guess that a lot of people don't think about why they exist. I don't happen to be one of these people. My existence involves continuing to verify that I do exist. My parents don't understand this method. So, I have decided to abandon identifying with my parents. Their views do not help me.

Philosophy, on the other hand, helps a little.

October 28, 2004

I do not love myself. A depressing notion but also one not worth being depressed over. Instead, I am angry. I am beyond furious. The negativity of self-detest is poison. I've been bled dry. Instead of feeling comfort in my emptiness, I want to flee. But being a student in university poses a commitment that I cannot seem to escape. So, I party on.

October 29, 2004

Depression remains a taboo topic. As does angst. I can sense others who suffer these afflictions of the mind. Maybe through a pained smile, a sarcastic joke, or a knowing glance.

Otherwise, we all hide.

Hidden, no real dialogue is exchanged with those around me. Words go right through us and nothing registers.

October 31, 2004

Isolation is teaching me a little bit about Love. I am starting to form an opinion on what it is, based on knowing what it isn't.

November 5, 2004

I contemplate killing myself every day at the moment. And every day, I decide not to. I decide that it's not worth it. Not worth losing the vision of who I have the potential to be.

Between who you are and who you have the potential to be seems to be where there is hope.

November 7, 2004

During these trips to the ocean, to Tofino, I feel something. The energy from the waves and the rain washes over me. For a moment everything is beautiful. Everything is perfect.

November 8, 2004

Somewhere behind the blank stare is a smile. It crept up when Skull Bus Matt told me he was willing to miss a session in the waves to hang out. That he knew I needed cheering up. Even though I had no future beyond that day with him, this made me feel special. However, since it seems I have a crush on a different guy every couple of weeks, this smile will fade. I won't properly smile until the smile comes from within.

November 13, 2004

There is an inherent sameness in all people. Everyone has to fight to survive in a crowded world with limited resources. Tools vary and the fitness to fight is not equal. Therefore, we adapt and use whichever tools are available. Everyone has a unique level of fitness and adaptability. This is where differences between individual people develop. We all need to play the cards we've been dealt in order to survive.

But to thrive, as opposed to merely survive, I think we must un-learn survival. Instead of feeling different, we must feel as one. With the universe and within.

November 15, 2004

Skull Bus Matt suggested coming to visit me at university. An unexpected development in our non-future together. I agreed to it after 48 hours of perusal. The corners of my mouth begin to lift. Then I receive a text saying that he needs dental work in Saskatoon and can't fit me in. Something about having limited leave from work. And an open-ended question about rescheduling for some time in the future. My smile fades. I can't even think ahead to tomorrow, let alone further away than that. So I plan to replace him. With another guy to impede the oneness I long for with the world at large. It makes me wonder, am I just as addicted to guys as I may be to drugs?

November 17, 2004
As if I need more impermanent smiles, Bryce momentarily paused his disregard for me to state that he enjoys my company and wants to hang out. Ironic, because I've been hanging out with Bryce's roommate. Who is kind, genuine, and hilarious. Exactly the opposite of Bryce.

November 20, 2004
If I want to actually improve my mental health, I should do more work in solitude.
Solitude failed.
I'm going to experiment with finding the right boyfriend to change my mood.
Being in Love has the power to heal. Maybe it can heal me.
The right guy is impossible to find.
So, instead, I will use any guy. Then convince myself to love him for whoever he is.

November 21, 2004
Any guy at this precise moment in time is someone named Tim. We sit beside one another in Biology. He is super tall and very cute. We enjoy talking. Tim wore a satin turquoise bowling jacket to compliment my turquoise stilettos. More importantly, Tim makes me feel good about myself. Not once have I broken down into tears beside him. Not once have I felt shredded to

pieces and wounded. Last night with him was amazing. A sensual exercise where I didn't feel disrespected or used.

I felt great.

*

November 22, 2004

Customers adore me as a waitress. My boss doesn't. This wasn't the formal reasoning she used for firing me, but I know it's the truth. Why this woman in her power cannot recognise me and help me overcome whatever work place issue I have is a question unanswered. If more women took the time to help develop other strong females, the world at large would face fewer dilemmas. I have no elder female role models right now. Instead, I am growing suspicious and full of malice. Such crippling emotions.

Effective today, I will refuse to hate or ridicule another woman solely because her youth or personality intimidates me. I can't force my ex-boss to change but I can be a part of the change someplace else. Within myself. And in the future.

November 25, 2004

I tried, again, with the best intentions, to talk to my parents. The conversation ran dry and I became annoyed. Curt, flippant responses are all I am capable of with them. Sadly, I cannot tell whether this is an improvement in relations or not.

November 27, 2004

I've been spending so much time outside of class with Tim that, on an experimental level, I lost the controls. Something powerful is going on. I can listen to him. I can actually hear him. Conversation between us flows and there appears to be minimal emotional drama. Even where my unhealthy personality is concerned, Tim's sound personality is a buffer. I feel stable and almost present. My inability to look forward, towards the future, does not plague me. Because in the actual moment, the here and now, I can go with the flow. My anxiety is reduced. And I like it.

November 28, 2004

Tim, who is the type of guy to take an extra minute to screen what he says to me – even in vulnerable moments, like when we're lying naked beside each other – doesn't break out any absurd comments. Instead, he is genuine. Something I prefer. Something I must have forgotten when I decided to go home with Bryce.

Drunk Bryce is a different person. He stops ignoring me. He becomes someone who likes to kiss me. In his domineering, dictator-like way he orders me to take off my clothes. I disobey. Instead I try to ask him personal questions. I want to explore his guarded emotional territory. To get any response from him, I slide on top of his body and caress his back and hair. This makes him shaky, nervous, and frustrated. After about ten minutes of this game, he is angry and withdraws from answering any further questions.

I tell Bryce that I know he is a good person. I want him to believe me. I say this because I want to believe it about myself.

*

December 2, 2004

Ashley looks at me. In the eyes. She says, I miss you.

Hearing this, I bound down the stairs away from the party into the seclusion of the laundry room. And cry.

The truth is, I miss her too.

Tim explains that when select people get to know our

weakest quality it creates the potential for that person to own those parts of us.

For this reason alone, nostalgia aside, I will never let Ashley back into my life. She knows that I am weak and that I can easily hurt innocent people.

December 13, 2004

I should be studying. Instead, I sleep. There is screaming in the silence that surrounds me. It scares me to realize that the events and people that occur in one's life shape it. If I were to take away these people and these events, I cannot conceptualize what my existence would be without them.

Lying in Tim's bed, I try to connect with him as two people in a moment of everything and nothing collided. This is so perfect and so beautiful that the moment extends. I almost forget my discontent. But then the moment runs out.

In silence I hold onto him tightly.

I hold on for dear life.

January 1, 2005

To bask in Tim's glory and pretend to have fun in the safety of the known will not allow me to grow. I want to grow. So I must leave Tim.

January 3, 2005

A tsunami just killed hundreds and thousands of people. I am not one of them.

January 4, 2005

Wasted. At the bar. Instead of talking to Tim to explain that I don't want to hang out anymore, I have amassed an entourage of five random guys. The beverage this evening, care of Brenna, is

The Special Cuervo. A mixture of vodka, wine, dried strawberries plucked from Kellogg's Special K cereal, Cuervo tequila, and margarita mix.

I decide to leave with one of the five. His apartment, decorated in beer boxes, smells like cat pee. His roommate just spilled water from a water bong onto my coat. The stench of hundreds of old marijuana cigarettes will leave with me. Why can't I find more places to spend time at that smell wonderful?

January 10, 2005

At Brenna's I see something. A scrapbook titled Natural Highs. One day I want to live like that. On a natural high.

January 18, 2005

A group of want-to-be lawyers, and myself. Collectively, we pretend to be diplomatic representatives of various countries and international organizations in a role-playing effort. To share ideas about how to save the world. This is Model United Nations.

To fit in with this group I smoke weed. Not because anyone else is smoking but because it makes this sort of acting more humorous. Unfortunately, smoking marijuana is also linked to accelerated aging and cancer. THC may be considered by some as medicinal. Part of me thinks that it helps with depression and craziness. But the side-effect, paranoia, may not be worth the benefits.

January 21, 2005

When uni roommate Nicole meets a guy she decides how to act around him based on whether he is one-night quality versus whether he is lobster quality. According to her, lobsters mate for life. According to her, if we like someone and want to hang out more than once we must act differently than if we just want to

33

hang out for one night. I have a problem planning my behaviour accordingly. Seems I am a bad lobster.

January 23, 2005
I made a painting. It is of a distorted female body lying on a beach among a bed of hibiscus flowers. The waves are raging. In the horizon a pack of wild horses run against a blazing sunset. This painting must be me.

The woman in it is malformed.

January 26, 2005
I chug a beer.

Then another.

Some varsity runner and I leave the humid bar. Inside his home he pours an orange juice and hands it to me. We sit on the edge of his bed. He pats the mattress to his right then lies down and says, it's sleepy time.

I'm in a headlock, while he snores lightly in my ear. I'm fully clothed. I wonder what I'm doing wrong.

*

February 20, 2005
There is an emerging state of uncertainty and fear that something catastrophic is about to happen. I try to avoid making any statements that imply a commitment of the mind, to respect the extreme fluctuation in my emotions.

The future continues to give me intolerable anxiety. I wonder if my classmates notice this. I sit in Psychology and consider. I close the binder that I have been drawing in and stare into space. Classroom lighting is always so white. I fidget with my pen. A decision forms in my mind. After class I am I going to visit the campus hospital and see a psychiatrist. My behaviour: always late, frequently absent, and fidgeting too much. I know that I drink too much coffee. But something else is the problem. Things have gotten worse for me. I skipped my last midterm. I lied about why. Overall, I feel horrible.

It is conceivable that I am studying psychology because I require psychiatric help. This must be a natural progression for anyone learning about this field. I leave the seminar and walk through cut grass to a clinic set amongst tall trees. Inside, I tell a doctor that I'm not sure why I'm here. He hands me a sheet of paper. I fill it out. As honestly as possible. Then I walk back across the field into the SU building and slide another paper across a counter. After five minutes a few vials appear. Pills to help with depression and anxiety.

I like to think that long-term cognitive behavioural therapies can come later. Pills claim that they offer a more immediate solution. So I open the vials and take a mixture of everything. Thirty minutes go by and I don't feel any differently.

February 25, 2005

I am convinced that taking several prescriptions at once will help get me through the next couple of months. I haven't told anyone about these meds because of factors like Brenna's book on Natural Highs.

No one respects drugs. Not ones taken to avoid being high. Like the ones I am taking to try to become more stable.

February 27, 2005

Are you prepared for something incredible?

I found myself scrawling this on the hem of my friend's tank top as we migrated to a pyjama party last night. One day this phrase will be necessary.

35

March 11, 2005

My friend Andre slipped on beer and broke his arm at the Super Bowl party. Because of this he is going eastward to Calgary to get surgery. This is an opportunity to pile my things inside his van, drive 14 hours, and show up on my brother's doorstep. This is my new plan for after graduation. I am going to move to a new city.

March 16, 2005

I upped the dosage of the stabilizer I'm on. Or maybe it's the antidepressant. After putting all of the prescriptions into an old black film container to make them more discreet, I can no longer tell the difference.

March 22, 2005

My friend Enzo, with the insane big blue eyes, is systematically re-introducing me to cocaine. I like them both in their own way. Enzo and the cocaine. Together, Co-Kenzo. High, we're magnetic. And not a popular combination. Likely, because he has a proper girlfriend. Also, playing haphazardly with magnetism, the strongest force is going to demagnetise the weakest.

March 25, 2005

Even though I am about to have a university degree, I also like my current work as a hostess at an Irish pub. It is the type of job that involves a lot of standing around, smiling, and slamming black coffee. My bosses are all men and they encourage me.

As a shiny bronze mindless tartan miniskirt, I feel absolutely nothing. This may have to do with the prescription drug cocktail. But then again, maybe not.

All I'm certain of is uncertainty itself.

March 29, 2005

I was feeling rather bland, beige, and boring but got my groove back. Which I owe to marijuana.

A joint hangs off my lower lip.

April 1, 2005

Aristotle once said that we can measure virtue in accordance with reason. Knowing myself today, if Aristotle were feeling generous, he would tell me that I am far more virtuous than reasonable. And I'm OK with that.

April 3, 2005

The more time I spend with Co-Kenzo, the more people question why.

Well, to find out what you want in life, it helps to identify that which you don't. Flirting in this direction suits my life because I have lost my appetite for anything else. Most days I do not have an answer to why I should even get out of bed. So, if Nicole isn't around, I don't. My textbooks refer to this sort of behaviour as depression. I disagree. This is boredom.

April 17, 2005

I finished my final tests. To celebrate, I smoke a joint. With each toke the giant pendulum that lives inside me swings. Afterwards, I feel content. I hold onto this as long as I can. I take a picture of it. Just like all the memories of the amazing friends I met in these past years at school. Some of whom I will stay in contact with. Some of whom will become nothing more than a distant memory. I'm scared that this feeling of content will become distant too.

April 18, 2005

I woke up in an unfamiliar condo. It's inhabited by a fellow player of Model United Nations. He had been assigned the Bahamas. I was at work for Bahrain. Right now we hope we're in Canada.

At the door is a bag full of CDs that we must have stolen from the DJ. My playmate looks a disaster. I dread to think of his review of me.

Over bottled water we discuss how neither of us remembers getting home. A feeling more eerie than the usual blackout drunk looms in the air. It tells me to stop mixing prescription sleeping pills with alcohol.

May 1, 2005
Graduated from university, I'm on the way towards a pink horizon.

Brenna is the last person I spoke to before leaving. She imparted solid words about moving on. She says, always leave on a high note. This way one can remain, in the mind of another, an oasis of perfection.

I turn towards Andre, beside me in his van. My baggage out of sight in the back. His limp arm hangs between us like a reminder of the falls we take along the way.

I place one of the anxiolytics under my tongue.

Happiness, according to these pills, is chemical.

26

||||| ||||| ||||| ||||| |

*"Some things in life are easy to get into.
And these very things are the hardest to get out of."*

May 3, 2005

Calgary spelt in another language is P-A-R-T-Y. One place for this is another Irish pub, Ceili's. Here, all the girls have rounded fake breasts and all the men act crazy. Across the bar, I'm lying on my back. The bartender free pours tequila directly into my mouth. I dance, just like this. Lying across the bar.

My friend tugs at my skirt because she wants to go. I descend and grab her hand. We run out the door and into the first yellow cab in sight. There's a man sitting in the front passenger seat. I explain that it's my first night on the town. He directs the taxi to a hotel and invites us in. We follow.

At the ATM machine he inserts his card and asks me to punch in some numbers.

I press the five.

He adds two zeros.

The notes appear and he smiles, placing them gingerly into my hands. Welcome to Calgary.

May 14, 2005

I'm thinking of taking a job at a weight loss clinic. Not one that recommends exercise. Just designer food and a cleanse that consists of green vegetables and some kind of special juice. The owner told me during the interview that in order to work here I have to cleanse. In order to empathize with the clientele.

In my hand is a giant bottle of burnt orange-coloured liquid. A fluid that runs straight through me. I call this poop juice.

Instead of following the juice diet for just one week, I do it for two. My fridge is full of spinach and broccoli.

May 15, 2005

I decide that being skinny is important. But also that a bar job is a better career move than a weight loss clinic.

The manager of the bar where I'm going to work goes over the different beers on tap. I stand in fluorescent pumps, fluorescent make-up, feather earrings, two padded push up bras, and a miniskirt. I look at my colleague, then at my manager. Across the bar three guys sit in a row drinking tall ones. Eenie, Meenie, Miney, Moe.

The scene around here will not involve poop juice.

May 17, 2005

I went home with one of the other bartenders. Before anything could happen he called me muffin and I started to cry. I don't know why I am crying. I don't even know who I'm crying for. Myself? The universe? Everyone else out there who feels as unloved as I do? Clearly I do not want to be called muffin.

Clearly the antidepressants are garbage.

May 18, 2005

In fact, none of my pills seem to work any longer. If they ever did. My skin feels like it is crawling over my bones. Floating, maybe. Inside, I feel hopeless. Whether absence of hope points to an external state or an internal one depends on where hope itself originates from.

Something I have long forgotten.

May 20, 2005

I thought a new city would be the right path. I came here looking to feel stronger and more together. To feel something, anything, more. Instead I feel completely vapid, empty, and alone.

Bartending doesn't help.

I stand behind a piece of furniture. The wood, we call it. In front of me stand (or sit) anywhere from one single businessman enjoying a pint over his lunch to dozens of savage maniacal drunks. No matter who looms on the other side, they all want something from me. I like the power this affords. Being able to decide who to serve, how to prepare their poison, and in what manner to present myself (or not).

Aside from the social experiment, the sad thing about this environment is that even in the middle of a party, which I'm often orchestrating and definitely facilitating, I feel totally isolated.

Life with my brother isn't any more comforting. Part of me hoped that being with him at this time would provide me with some answers. About why I am the way I am. I look at his blue eyes and blonde hair, in contrast to my brown eyes and raven hair. Perhaps we are more different than we are similar.

My brother does not seem to suffer from emotional turbulence.

May 22, 2005

Some people hitchhike as a cheap mode of physical transport. To get from A to B. I see it as an opportunity to meet people.

Standing outside Cowboys nightclub after closing time and showing a lot of leg, I do my own version.

A black Hummer pulls up. The unnecessarily huge vehicle provides a fitting foreshadow for the events to come. The door opens and a tanned and curvaceous brunette asks if I want to come to an after party.

Two men sit in the front seats. I can tell by their chunky silver jewelry and gold-stitched, bedazzled T-shirts that they're the kind of guys who order Vodka Red Bull.

We drive to the suburbs of Calgary. A multitude of little boxes are splattered row-upon-row along streets that all go by the same name. Finally, we turn off from Riverside Boulevard onto Riverbend Close. We've arrived.

Inside, the walls are painted bright primary colours. Blue and yellow and red. A large leather furniture set and a 60-inch Sony flat screen TV eat the entire living room. It is evident that this home belongs to a man. In the kitchen people stand around the counter drinking vodka. Popular electronic music reverberates off the walls. No one is talking about anything interesting. Non-discreetly, baggies of cocaine haphazardly act as decor. A fake-tanned man lacking in neck is doing a line off a beige, oversized, square-shaped ceramic plate. As the cocaine invites me, another neckless man approaches. He hands over a one hundred dollar note.

I roll the bill, grab someone's gym membership card, and expertly push all the remaining flaked whiteness into a line the size of my finger.

Since people like to go big around here, I finish the rest of the coke in one successive inhale. The chemical aftertaste drips into a rapidly parched mouth as my heartbeat accelerates to match the song's tempo. Interrupting the moment, one of the bejewelled shirts wants to introduce me to the owner of the after party house.

A stocky and bald man of what I later learn to be Ukrainian descent approaches. His name is Denton, and apparently he's got the best drugs in town.

*

May 24, 2005

Denton stopped by the bar with some red pills. He calls them Red Rockets.

I took one.

My heart is beating so fast that I know I won't be sleeping tonight.

May 29, 2005

The end of May marks a holiday favourite. May Long. The long weekend was always an excuse to file off into the forest with a tent and your parents' car. Binge-drinking outdoors and camping were words interchanged.

Since none of my former friends are here, I do what seems reasonable and accompany Denton's baseball team to a tournament in the Okanagan.

I bid Calgary adieu.

Kelowna, a community that thrives off a large lake and wineries, is the destination. Some people call it the California of Canada, if such a comparison is possible. All I know is that this is my first time participating, as a spectator, in fastball. A sport kind of like baseball, with a different pitching style.

I'm hyper the whole ride and can't stop talking. The Red Rocket ephedrine pills have this effect. Enduring my chatter on the road alongside Denton is his brother, Garrett; a skinny heavy-duty mechanic from Saskatoon named Brian; and God.

Brian may be missing a few teeth but is rumoured to have one of the fastest underhand pitches in Western Canada. Denton is on three cell phones, sipping away at some beer, and speeding masterfully. Both Garrett and God sit silently, watching the landscape change as we wind along the mountainous highway.

Nearing Kelowna, out of nowhere, an airborne vehicle soars across the windshield. Denton stops to investigate. Shards of metal, glass, and crumpled wreckage indicate that the aircraft came from the opposite lane. Witnessing all this, God turns to look my way. Then, he walks away.

My heart is beating. Drumming, hard. Keeping a breakneck pace.

Onward. We decide to stop at Orchard Hill mall. The boys buy burgers. Denton offers me a line of cocaine, then we set off to MAC. New make-up is in order. Electric blue. Because I still feel electric.

May 30, 2005

Somerset Road. A street situated along the lake. A house party is before us. Nicole, who's working for the summer in Kelowna, is here waiting on the driveway.

We pass a pit bull and surveillance cameras at the front door. Inside, massive and terrifying people walk around. No one sees us.

This home may belong to a gang. The kind that ride around on motorcycles and manage strip clubs. Apparently, everyone is high on ecstasy. We infiltrate the crowd of sweaty, touchy-feely, scary people with big pupils. Loud electronic music blasts from surround sound speakers. Nicole looks at me and tells me to be careful. I can't hear her say this but can see it in her eyes. I turn to her and say that everything is fine, but I don't hear the words myself.

Back at the motel, an uneasiness descends. I can't recognise Denton. His face looks like an animal's. The door clicks shut and his expression changes again. Somehow his teeth are jagged and more pointy.

I try and dance past him towards the washroom but he grabs and hoists my body up into the air, his fingers clutching my thighs. From this angle he is leveraging me towards his face. I'm

44

terrified of those teeth. With one hand I awkwardly brace the ceiling and with the other hand, his shoulder. My body is on his mouth.

He throws me face-first onto the bed. Then his fangs attack. I'm screaming. Or maybe not. In any event, his animal instincts don't listen. His hands and body smother me. A predator devouring its prey. I fear any movement at all will break my neck. My head, at an unnatural angle, houses my mind in panic. I clench my teeth into the mattress and close my eyes. This is rough.

In the morning, with the safety of sunlight, I exit onto the balcony. It could be the right time to take up smoking cigarettes. Brian is outside having one and looks in my direction. Without speaking, I can tell he knows that I am wondering if I got raped last night.

May 31, 2005

I help myself to more cocaine. Around me are families. People who look nothing like me. I can't look at these people. Especially not at the children.

After baseball we go to a strip club where someone orders food and a plate of it ends up in front of me. The liquid that glazes the skin of the chicken wings is like paint. I use my finger to trace it around the white table setting. On cocaine it is impossible to eat food. I pick up a single French fry, and chew and chew and chew. After a hundred chews, I swallow. My heart is beating so fast. The same person who brought the food brings a bright red Caesar. A combination of Clamato, vodka, Tabasco, and Worcestershire sauce. The drink is gone within seconds.

My jaw is clenched.

Brian leans over and tells me that I do not have to be alone with Denton again tonight.

I want to make a more dramatic statement.

Back at the motel, in the bed opposite Denton, I lie on my side. My eyes are wide open. I breathe through my mouth and stare across the small space at Denton. He stares back at me. Behind me, Brian is pressed against my body. He is holding me. He is warm. He is gentle. He is exactly the type of person I would want to have sex with.

So I do.

Denton stares at us.

No one says anything.

Denton continues to stare.

June 1, 2005

With the next source of daylight, Brian is gone. According to Denton he had a plane to catch. I can tell this arrangement was not by choice. The entire ride back, I have nothing left to say.

From now on everyone I like is long gone. And so am I.

*

June 10, 2005

To say that I stopped hanging out with Denton would be nice. If it were true.

He drives me around. Takes me to dinner. Brings me Red Rockets. Slips me some money here and there. And, he's got all the coke.

June 17, 2005

Instead of asking, I steal bags of blow from inside the truck. There are always a few grams or half grams tucked inside a black sports sock within arm's reach of the front passenger seat.

June 18, 2005

Sleep isn't important to me.

Sleepless, I prefer the inside of a dark nightclub. There's a party going on every night of the week in Calgary. Monday is Ceili's. Tuesday is the Speakeasy. Wednesday is the Back Alley. Thursday is Coyotes. Friday and Saturday is Cowboys. And Sunday is the Mynt. This is exactly how my schedule goes. My existence. A state of semi-heart attack and clubbing.

From all the extra sleep I got in past years, maybe I built up a reserve of energy. I plan to now spend it as fast as I can.

June 20, 2005

Life continues to revolve around little plastic bags of cocaine, nail and hair extensions, tanning, and bartending. This schedule has alienated me from most people, including my brother. I don't want to meet anyone new. Instead, I watch movies. Movies don't ask any questions.

I am watching one at Denton's as the doorbell rings. Some people I recognise from the gym are standing out front. They are here for a juice jug that's in the cupboard. A jug filled with water. But it isn't water.

One of the gym guys tells me it's G. He tells me I should try some because it will make me skinny and toned.

Denton tells me I'm not allowed any G. He says it's too addictive for girls. I don't know if I believe him.

June 21, 2005

I am speaking to Desha, a former stripper who seems to now get by cleaning houses.

She has a fantastic ass. Her face though, which is really pretty, looks like it has seen and done things that have taken a toll. Upon closer inspection, she looks crooked.

It turns out that she's Denton's proof that G is bad for women. She drank some one night driving home and fell unconscious behind the wheel. The crash sent her through the windshield. When the police and ambulance arrived, she was busted. Both in the face and for transporting drugs.

I can tell Desha has changed but I can't tell if she's happy or not. She must know things. About recovery. And for this reason I am glad to have met her.

June 25, 2005

I met another girl who's staying at Denton's house. Drop-dead gorgeous and in the midst of running away from her ex-boyfriend. A half-Iranian guy who just got out of jail. I met him once in a parking lot. If he was my boyfriend, I'd be trying to run away too.

Girls like her seldom get very far though. Some things in life are easy to get into. And these very things are the hardest to get out of.

June 27, 2005

Denton has a day job consulting operators on how to protect their pipelines in the oil field. This whole city is fed off the oil and gas industry. I encourage him to focus on that job instead of the other one. Drug dealing.

*

June 28, 2005

I started by having drinks with my manager but woke up somewhere else. My clothes are on the floor. There is a condom wrapper on the nightstand.

My manager's in bed beside me.

48

Some people call this being taken advantage of. If I could remember anything, I'd have an opinion on that.

June 29, 2005

No one understands why I quit my job before the city-wide party called Stampede, which is the best time to make money bartending. No one understands why I can't work there anymore. Money or not.

I can't possibly be in the same building as my former manager.

July 3, 2005

Across a boardroom table is a man named Gene. I think he's half Asian. His fake British accent confuses people. At his side is another man, Mr. Lightstone. These two men are interviewing me for a sales job. My attire looks more suitable for a nightclub. All I can think about is those of us present in a lurid threesome on the boardroom table. It is large enough to accommodate that sort of thing.

Either owing to or despite my cleavage, they offer me a job. In the elevator, a soon-to-be colleague tells me that sometimes after work they have drinks in the boardroom then head out for more drinks on a patio somewhere nearby. As long as this patio is not the one at the place where I used to work, it all sounds like fun. And perhaps it's possible to convince the management about my ideas concerning the boardroom table.

July 6, 2005

I am going to a wedding. With Denton.

When I think of weddings, I picture having drinks somewhere where a couple is getting married, doing some coke, and going to a club afterwards. This particular wedding is nothing like what I had in mind.

The venue is a private estate on a ranch and the other women are wearing floor-length gowns. I am wearing a tube top, as a dress.

Denton is not impressed. He makes it clear that I look like a slut.

I want to tell him that if people don't like my attire then they don't have to look at me. No one seems to be looking anyway.

The surroundings are far too beautiful. The glistening crowd is gathering to mingle in an open field. Beside some rose bushes a harpist plays classical music. A glass of champagne and some canapés from a well-groomed young man in a long tuxedo and top hat make their way into my hands. Quickly, the music changes and the bride and groom emerge.

After a five-minute ceremony the couple is man and wife. I see white doves flutter into the blue sky. The standing crowd turns to face the lovers. We raise our champagne glasses.

I've secretly been drinking vodka at the bar. I'm hammered. And dying to get out of here. I wonder where I can get some blow. The seventy-five-year-old man in front of me asking which island in the Caribbean I prefer does not seem a reliable source. I down another glass of vodka and sneak off. In the washroom I call my new boss Gene to see what he is up to tonight. Maybe he likes to party.

With the phone still in hand, I walk out the door and into Denton. He is livid. Despite our surroundings, the words exchanged between us are far from quiet. I lament that Denton is right. I shouldn't be drunk dialing my boss.

From this perspective, the dirt road back to civilization is long.

We're not waiting around for any of the arranged transportation. At a brisk pace, with a firm grip on my arm, Denton makes away from the property with me in tow. To keep up, I consider taking off my heels and bare-footing it. By now, his other hand is in my hair. My feet aren't running alongside him anymore. I'm being dragged along the dirt road.

Finally, a cab intervenes. Inside, panic overcomes me. I'm genuinely terrified of Denton.

Understandably, the driver does not wish to get involved. With us in the back he proceeds slowly and does not glance at the mayhem. At us. Denton is slurring. He is threatening to not pay the cab fare and threatening me with worse. I scream at the cab driver to take me to a police station or my brother's house. We arrive at the latter and I make a run for the front door.

Deadbolt in place, I tell my brother what just happened and then pick up the phone. This time I don't call my boss. I call Denton and tell him we're over. I mean it.

Drunk and probably stoned and bewildered. My feet are bleeding and my scalp hurts. Denton's response is firm.

No.

We are not done.

If I think I'm going to walk away from him and walk around town freely, I have another thing coming. His words, not mine.

*

July 10, 2005

I run my fingers through my long flat-ironed locks and try to remember the person I used to be. This might be necessary to have fun with some friends from university who are here to party. We are going on a pub crawl. In my purse are several grams of cocaine. I'm not sure if this will help or hinder the events to come.

July 11, 2005

I wake up with Enzo in my bed. Co-Kenzo. Since I'm late for work, I don't have time to reflect.

All this partying has taken a toll and I am plagued. By the fact that nothing in my life feels the same. Not my old friends. Not my old flings. Not even myself.

Nothing is the same anymore.

July 16, 2005

Denton knows about Enzo. I have no idea how. He imparted this knowledge after dropping me off at the STD clinic.

July 21, 2005

A wet paintbrush, held high, looks like a sword. The walls are turquoise. There is paint splattered all over the window, the carpets, and my clothing. I painted my bedroom. A final effort to remind myself of who I used to be.

Inside this bright blue asylum, I can't stop crying. It's been days since anyone spoke to me. Blue is the colour of the energy centre in our throat. It governs activities like communication.

I have no one to talk to. My brother moved out. In a few weeks I have to leave as well. Our lease is over.

July 25, 2005

At work I got a promotion because I'm fierce at telemarketing. Though a small success it is incapable of easing the growing concern about my personal life. My colleagues seem to think that Denton is stalking me. I try not to talk about things like this. But part of me wants to.

August 4, 2005

In a leather bomber jacket and gold lightning bolt earrings I should feel safe. I don't. Denton and I flew to Vancouver for a weekend away. Or so I thought. At the hotel he asked me to call Enzo. To arrange a meeting.

He tells me that no one will find out. That he plans to kill him.

I have no idea if he is insane or joking. I have no idea of anything. Words do not come out of my mouth. My mind changes to a new channel. I decide to try to ignore what is happening. Denton gets in the shower and I investigate the contents of his duffel bag. Inside are some pills. I retrieve seven of them. Popping two, the rest I put in my purse for safe keeping.

Slowly, reality changes. The current channel, of ignoring a murder plot, is replaced with something else. Vibrations and colour.

I no longer recognise anything. Not my speech. Not my old friends that I run into in the streets. Not even my own face.

I am surging. Either towards heaven or towards hell. Whatever the direction, I don't care. Because these pills take me away from here. Towards the fireworks.

I am flying.

August 6, 2005
After we fly with artificial wings, we crash. I plummeted to a new low.

I no longer feel anything at all.

25

||||| ||||| ||||| ||||| ||

"Jealously wears a face that I cannot stomach to look at."

August 10, 2005
Along with the departure, my brother announced that he doesn't want me coming around. He hasn't told me his new address.

August 20, 2005
Lying in the grass at a park in Sunnyside, the air is cool. Summer is over and I'm trying to envision what it will be like to be homeless in a few days. Autumn leaves bury my soul. Soon it will be too cold to lie outside like this. Since I haven't found a new place to live, I will need a plan. My brother is gone and so is my last stash.

Across 10th Avenue NW, I see people inside a bar. My body walks in. Immediately, a man is asking if I'm OK. Who knows what gave it away. I tell him the truth. That I'm out of coke.

He looks at me, smiling, then slides a flap along the bar and into my palm.

August 21, 2005
I am running past my body. A body that stands at the side of the road as Denton's truck pulls up.

I stop and watch her get in. I want to turn away and keep running. Instead I listen. She asks to move in with him.

He says yes.

Then I run. Not in the opposite direction but towards the car. In the glove compartment I find the black sock, slip my hand inside, and grab whatever miniature plastic bags I can.

September 2, 2005
In time to celebrate our cohabitation at Denton's, his house got broken into. We pulled up to broken glass beside the front door. His safe is missing.

A short, fat middle-aged thug arrives to suggest that I executed the robbery. No one trusts my denial of this.

No one trusts me.

Myself included.

September 17, 2005
Because I asked, Gene told me that I am allowed to bring a dog to work. Having a dog means having someone to talk to. Uncensored.

September 18, 2005
The domestic fights continue to escalate to new levels. Lately, I see nothing but red. Then I see Bobby. Our current roommate. He is standing between us asking calmly for me to go into the washroom.

Detached, I listen and oblige. Then I hear Bobby tell me to lock the door. So I do.

Things are thrown around. Things are broken. Malicious words are uttered. I sit on the cold slate floor and wait for the red to disappear. Bobby is the only person who will intervene in these fights. No one else dares. I don't like fighting but it is impossible not to. This time I caught Denton going through my phone. Which is how he found out about Enzo. And everything else.

September 20, 2005

I'm doing a bump off the toilet paper dispenser at work.

Exiting the stall, a cotton-mouthed wreck emerges. Cocaine is no longer a pleasant or sexy high for me.

It is a mind-numbing wave of paranoia. Aversive. For this reason alone, I need it.

Back at my desk, the man who sits in the cubicle beside mine looks at me. Like he knows what I'm up to. I decide that it is only a matter of time before I have to quit.

Not the coke, but my job.

September 26, 2005

At the house there is another drug. Also a white powder but glassier than cocaine. More crystal.

That's also what it's called.

Sometimes it is separate. And other times is gets mixed in.

Entire days can go by. Later, when you're done, you don't look human anymore. Definitely not like the person you started as.

I'm sure I've lost about twenty pounds. Not that I weigh myself. My cheekbones tell me this. Clothes fall off my waist. So I wear the same Lulu Lemon black stretch pants for days at a time. I do not wash my hair. I do not wear make-up. I smell like chemical death.

But, somehow, I am alive.

October 15, 2005

The only plan I have is working. Project dog. I found one on the Internet. She's a Japanese Chin. A toy. I'm going to name her Sushi. She is going to save my life.

October 25, 2005

In the middle of the night two men with garbage bags full of marijuana come by to repackage it. From upstairs I try to ignore them. Unfortunately I can't. The humming of a table-top vacuum sealer rings in my ears. Enough is enough. I scream at them to get out.

Hidden in my draw is a couple thousand dollars that they left behind. Consolation money I took to accomplish my latest project.

October 31, 2005
A dog is my angel of change.

November 5, 2005
Without a locked safe, I am a cat burglar who lives freely on the inside. This analogy explains the crawling around on the carpeted floor in the basement looking for drug-like debris. Looking for a clue to where a larger stash is hidden. It's always hidden somewhere. I just don't know where.

A panel from the wall shelving unit is loose. It pops off. Inside I reach my hand and feel the package. Score. With my hands bare I use my fingers to scrape chunks of blow into my palm. I stand up and spread the chemical whiteness onto a linoleum counter top and continue to separate it into something I can put into my nose. On the floor beside me Sushi waits. She's sniffing at something. Then she eats a chunk.

Her eyes bulge out with disgust and she spits it out. I am motionless. My heart stops. Cocaine would kill her. Equally disturbing, I am about to put something into my body that is so obviously toxic that not even a dog will take it.

This cunning kitty, who always finds what she's looking for, starts to look for something else.

An escape.

*

November 7, 2005

I set out to discover truths in the world. And I did. One hard truth stares at me through an agitated face in the mirror. I look rough. What it is like to be a mental prisoner. To be a drug addict. The lines across my forehead beg me to put on the brakes. But with white lines, I speed forward. Caught somehow motionless in acceleration. Movement never felt so still. I wonder how much faster I can go. The stillness of full speed will save me from this prison. My forehead, pursed, begs me to fix the brakes and take my heart out of this race. My heart is willing to walk away. Into the cold, dark night.

Another one I will not be sleeping through.

November 13, 2005

During the especially bad fights I call the police. This is my response to intense violence. I am scared and I am angry and my anger wants backup. I hang up the phone. The tension in the air is thick enough to cut. Neither of us says anything. Not Denton. Not me. We are in silence and everything is red. I imagine what it's like to look him in the eyes. His home address is known so response comes quickly. The doorbell rings and two male officers enter. They ask what the disturbance is. They are speaking to me. But their words are fake. A memorised speech, impersonal and cold. This is called protocol.

My mouth will not open. It can't. The thickness of the tension outweighs my ability to speak. Finally, I shift my gaze to these officers and try to tell them everything through my eyes. That I need help. That I need to get out of this house. But my mouth disobeys.

My mouth tells them that nothing is wrong. That I made a mistake.

The police respond, cutting the tension into a million pieces.

A million pieces that I choke on. I have wasted their time. They are furious. Gasping for air, I stare at the officer closest to me. I expect him to resuscitate me. He ignores the million pieces of tension, ignores my gasps for air. Instead, he looks at me in contempt and tells me once more that this is a waste of time.

Denton doesn't look at me. He takes three strides through the tension with confidence and tells the policemen to get out of his house. They listen. They are gone. The red fades.

To black.

November 19, 2005

I love Denton. A year ago I thought Love was something warm. Something gentle and unspoken. Given by someone like Tim who listens tirelessly. By someone like my mother who feels my every emotion. And there is love like that. Warm and gentle. But the love I know right now is hard. Hard and tragic. The love I know today is about jealousy, disrespect, anger, control, and compulsion.

I want to escape this tragic love.

The most available option is to run away with one of Bobby's friends, an exotic dancer named Kitty Kat Casey. She is exactly like her name. Bouncy and fun. She is exactly like what I am not.

I dress for the role. In a miniskirt, I am prepared to flee.

Before I can exit the front door Denton demands that I change my clothing. I refuse. This elicits a stare down. The tension between us begins to grow. I attempt to storm out the door anyway. But instead my body is in the air. Over Denton's shoulder. He is carrying me upstairs. I begin kicking and attempt to climb off him but the tension and his strength have more power than my limbs. He puts me down in front of the closet and repeats his request that I change. Head down I attempt again to dodge in protest. But I can't get by. His chest and body and the tension block me. I bounce. From inside the bedroom I hear Casey and Bobby leaving. I hear the front door close.

Then I hear the bedroom door close and lock from the outside. They have left this house for the night. I have been locked in and left behind.

November 20, 2005
I hurt. Deep inside.

November 21, 2005
I wait for the G to kick in. To bring me to sleep. I don't care if Denton finds out I'm on G. I need some poison stronger than the poison of uncertainty and jealously and pity and hopelessness that rages inside me. Jealously wears a face that I cannot stomach to look at.

I am sick from this face and explore getting even sicker. My vision goes and so does my ability to speak. I hear a strain of slurred words emit from my body. This is the sound of Gamma-Hydroxybutyrate. GHB. A drug that can make your heart stop beating after you pass out from it. A consequence I welcome.

*

November 24, 2005
Strapped inside the engine of the truck is a medium-sized package of drugs. Denton and I are driving to deliver it to a man who owns a gym in a small town in southern Saskatchewan. This is called drug trafficking. This is also called Thanksgiving long weekend. A concept that does not fit into any category of my current repertoire. Around me are the prairies. A flat, vast landscape that is so uninterrupted. The opposite of me.

I find beauty in this surrounding.

Beyond our vehicle are bales of hay, a red barn with white trim, and a blue sky. A sky that stretches far away to the heavens of another world. This weekend will be my first taste of rehab. Of sobriety. I have promised myself no hard drugs. The thought of this makes me feel sick. And antisocial. I'll wear my sunglasses. Even as night befalls the prairies around us.

A bottle of Red Rockets calls me. I pop one after another. These are not hard drugs. The blue and silver can of Red Bull also calls me. I drink it. My heart matches the speed of the truck. 170 kilometres per hour. In the rear-view mirror red and blue lights flash. This is the police. I do not remove my sunglasses and no one looks at me. No one looks under the hood. Without asking questions they exchange Denton his ID for a speeding ticket. Somehow all this speed is arousing. The police, too, turn me on. A sentiment that reminds me that I'm still here.

Otherwise, I remain long gone.

November 25, 2005

An alarming scream pierces the empty farmland. I freeze. In front of me a husky has my dog in his mouth. Sushi. The husky whips his head to the side. A movement to snap Sushi's neck. The piercing scream rips my heart in half. It is coming not from my mouth but from the mouth of my little dog. I do not scream because I am frozen. Denton flies on top of the husky and grabs him in a headlock. My dog is crying. Like a baby. I pick her up in my arms and everything becomes silent.

This is a reminder that I have to be alert. My dog just almost died.

*

December 10, 2005

In a pink bag from Holt Renfrew is a floor-length black and gold designer gown and golden sparkly shoes. A Christmas bonus. The dress is a size 0. The same number as my confidence to wear such an item.

December 14, 2005

I am at the gym, on the stair climber. One of the trainers is walking towards me. I don't know where to look. I don't know what to say to him. Before I can say nothing, he puts his hand beside mine on the machine's black handlebar and asks me to go home.

The gym management wants me to go home.

The mirrors that line the wall in front of us shatter. I run into the ladies change room. The mirrors here are shattered worse. I stand on the scale. It says 89 lbs. I want to turn around and announce that I'm not here to lose weight. I want to announce that this gym is a refuge.

Instead of explaining anything, I choke on saliva. It drips from the corner of my mouth and blends with my tears. I rinse this fluid away with cold water and slide sunglasses over my eyes. I walk past the management, up the stairs, and into a tremendously bleak night.

December 26, 2005

People around me are shopping. On the escalator, descending, my heart stops. Everything is literally black. The pain in my chest is real. The blackness around me is real. I clutch the side rails and calmly tell Denton that I need to go to the emergency room.

In slow motion, I arrive at the Foothills hospital. Beyond the double sliding doors I collapse on the floor. Either naturally or melodramatically. At this point I have no idea. My eyes stare at three specks of gravel and a small pool of brown liquid. The remnants of snow, dirtied, tracked inside and melted on the waiting room floor.

I can hear noises. They seem to be coming out of my mouth. I want attention and I want it now. Someone comes and lifts me off the floor and carries me past dozens of eyes. Dozens of waiting eyes stare at me in this horrible room. Triage.

Tonight I cannot just sit and wait. A realisation that causes a small earthquake of sobbing in my body. The movement reveals that I'm not dead. I hate needles. And I hate that no one here feels sorry for me. I have brought myself to the hospital on a cocaine overdose.

A drugs overdose is a slap in the face, and also my current reality.

Gradually, the trembling stops. The pain in my chest is as hard as a rock. The nurse looks at me. I do not tell her how much cocaine I have been using or where I get it from. I explain to her that cocaine is not my biggest problem. That I have others. Namely, the battle I've waged against myself. Life, I want to tell her, is like this. You are your biggest enemy and, also, a potential champion.

Cocaine is just something that happens along the way. The nurse asks if I want treatment. Beside her a doctor repeats the question. Do I want to go to an addiction recovery treatment facility? I say nothing because the answer is No.

No one asks any further questions. I listen to a dialogue, its delivery robotic. More protocol. I feel a glimmer of light. A choice is presented to me. To intervene on how pathetic I have become or to die. I think about responsibility. About my dog at home. This is the reason I will not go to the formal rehabilitation programme proposed. Because this facility does not accept pets. I am confident in my decision because it is the same rationale

I exercised two weeks ago when I refused to go to a women's shelter. They don't accept pets there either.

Before taking me home, Denton makes sure to stop at an ATM. My bank card's inserted into the machine to withdraw money from my account. A businessman, he is. Collecting payment for the goods his secret customer has been using.

December 27, 2005

In a floor-length designer gown people notice me. People seemed to notice me all night. Up until moments before Denton got arrested. That is precisely when people stopped noticing me. When Denton got arrested for battering me in public. Then no one seemed to notice.

Party-goers at a swanky Christmas do for an oil and gas company do not want to see violence. They only want to see the glimmering person standing behind the chocolate fondue fountain. Beyond the smell of chocolate is the smell of new money. The price of oil is at an all-time high and these party-goers are happy. These party-goers are rich.

My gold sparkly high heels walk towards the server. He hands me a glass of wine. My jewelry, make-up, and slicked up-do radiate glamour. I relish the escape of this escapade. My shoes keep walking. This time up to a man who's wearing a ten-gallon cowboy hat. I tell him what a fantastic hat he has. Denton is alarmed. Either by the fact that I'm having a good time, or that I'm drunk, or that I'm speaking to someone who happens to be a man.

Next thing I know, there is another man at Denton's side. He agrees that I am out of line. I am all alone and weak. Unprepared for a fight, the glittery shoes decide to make a run for it. Across the silent street to Denton's vehicle. Once there I change into pink suede sheepskin boots. Better traction. Tonight, I am prepared to liberate myself. Even if it means physically running away. I am prepared.

With my first stride, Denton is behind me. The trunk is open and I'm being pushed inside. Our struggle advances away from the trunk towards the passenger seat. My body is inside the vehicle, awkwardly stuffed into the footwell. My head is contorted and the seatbelt is wrapped around my shoulders.

Denton is sitting on me so I can't move. Finally, the seatbelt slacks. There are police approaching. They grab Denton off my body and handcuff him hard against the side of his SUV. Someone is explaining to me that the tinted windows prevented them from seeing clearly what happened. Since Denton was not in the driver's seat, he cannot be charged with drink driving. It is critical that I make a statement.

I am overwhelmed. Denton's beady eyes peer at me from the back of the police cruiser. Beady eyes that I am sick of. I am still prepared to run but the police stop me. They want to take me somewhere. All I know is that I want Sushi. My dog. The police explain that they want to take me to a shelter but that it doesn't allow animals. Of course. It dawns on me that I don't have anywhere to go. They ask about friends or family. I'm too ashamed to tell them how alone I've become.

The first name in my cell phone's contacts list is Brad. Someone I used to know. I call him.

He agrees to lend me his couch for the night. I listen to him call my dog a rat. I listen to alien laughter then leave at sunrise.

December 28, 2005
My feet walk across downtown to an office tower. The main entry is open. In the elevator, I go wherever it takes me. In this hallway I could be anywhere. The cold has gotten to my bones. Shivering, my phone rings. It's Denton. He's out of jail and

apologising for last night. I want to hang up. I want to use this as an excuse not to go back.

Deep inside I want to be someone strong. But instead, I feel like the word some people use as a description: a victim. I stare at this label, peel it off, toss it aside, and refuse to repeat it aloud. Then, I refuse to participate. For a fee, Denton's lawyer facilitates this. The non-participation. It took less than five minutes to sell myself out. Whatever the police want to do with Denton, I will not be involved.

The restraining order containing my name will be rescinded on the grounds that we work together. The phone continues to ring. The police, legal aid and victim's assistance unit are calling. A faceless voice tells me that my life is in danger. Somehow, this makes me smile.

I am my own worst enemy. Accordingly, it does not make sense to be scared of anybody else.

December 29, 2005
I am aware of how weak I have become. How much weight I have lost. It is evident by how people look at me. Bobby has another girlfriend over. I desperately want to go out with them and regain strength from the world that isn't here. But Denton is saying No. I am too drunk to go anywhere.

The base of the bottle of vodka in my hand tilts upwards. The remaining liquid goes down my throat. I put down the bottle and exchange it for a knife. This is my attempt at something dramatic. But before I can slice my body, everybody is on top of it. Denton, Bobby, the girl.

Under the dog pile, I pass out.

December 30, 2005
With significant condolence, I am not the only female around

66

here having a breakdown. There are innumerable others. Girls looking for drugs. They are drunk and they are absolutely crazy. From a leather chair in the living room I watch a catfight erupt. Half a T-shirt and three hair extensions adorn the floor. I see exactly what one step further in the direction I am headed in looks like.

I do not like it.

January 2, 2006

Denton took me to see my old friends, Brenna, Lana, and Tim. The four of us are in a hotel room. Everyone acts like things are normal. The steady and abundant supply of alcohol and marijuana encourages this. We avoid controversial conversation. I wear a miniskirt and bustier. Everything about me is exposed. Tim turns to me to say that I have more to offer the world. That I need to get out of my current situation. The Jägermeister within me responds. With how happy I am. Words which are slurred and nonchalant. Words that do not express how I actually feel.

This is how my night shall end. I am not strong enough for intimate conversation with real friends. I'm too ashamed.

January 3, 2006

Denton is not amused that Tim stayed the night. A point reiterated by his open hand and my stinging face. I no longer have a cell phone. And I can no longer justify our disturbing relationship.

24

||||| ||||| ||||| ||||| ||

"No matter where you run, there you are."

January 5, 2006

My parents flew me to their home. Each day that I'm away from Denton becomes a new day that I do not know myself.

My parents attempt to talk to me about drugs. What people don't understand is that my problem is not with drugs. It never has been. My problem is with myself. Sober.

Inside the beige office of a family doctor, my blood pressure and sonogram indicate that I am healthy. Deep inside, I know that I am not. I am hurting. I am hurt. The scars people like me are left with are deeper than can be revealed by any scale or stethoscope or blood test. The pathogens are not physical. They are psychological. Ultimately, it is the stream of wounded women I see around me who inspire me to quit. Because if I do not quit now, I know I risk permanent damage on the interior.

I feel guilty. Not for myself but for Denton. Because he still loves me. And I do not love him back.

I decide I need a vacation from this break.

January 9, 2006

I sit on the plane with my back to my parents and prepare to return to the unknown.

I am on my way towards not caring about the opinions of

others and towards surrounding myself with people that I respect. No more drug addicts. No more drug dealers. No more strippers. This will be a slow road from where I sit today.

An ascent of this magnitude will require more courage than protest. The largest protest is my denial. A strong defence mechanism exists inside us all. I did not realise but my deviation this past year has been a way to find courage. Self-humiliation along the way was unavoidable. There is nothing more humiliating than a battered drug addict.

I don't see the light at the end of the tunnel, but I do realise that I can't handle any more self-humiliation.

February 1, 2006

A friend of mine used to say that curiosity killed the cat but that satisfaction brought her back.

My mind is temptation. My mind causes me anguish. So I take to altering my mind. Doing this through drugs is a natural progression. I just happened to find the wrong one. The wrong ones. Ones that cause even more anguish, anxiety, and unnerving paranoia than any mind can find alone, unaltered. Cocaine is not euphoric. Instead it helps me to pass go and head straight to jail. To a low. This low is so uncomfortable that what I used to consider sadness or depression or anxiety or anger pales in comparison.

My addiction, right now, is not to any drug, but to pain.

This is proof that it is not possible to overdose on pain. Since physical pain and mental pain are two different kinds of pain, a sick mind can handle abnormal quantities of both kinds. Deep inside, I know I can overcome this. That my current reality is just a necessary stop. To truly know freedom, we must know it's opposite.

Mental prison.

February 9, 2006
I pour a small mountain of powder and cut it into three lines. Holding a short straw to my right nostril, I inhale it deeply.

The high actually hurts. It is the most high-strung, intense feeling that can possibly exist, naturally or even supernaturally.

I've learnt from this relapse that it is not enough to have good intention.

I need help.

February 10, 2006
Without intervention, I continue to sink into an illicit, killer binge. I accept that cocaine will be a struggle for some time. People cannot trust me with any quantity of this drug. And that includes myself.

My shoulders and neck are tense. I sip on Grey Goose and wait for sleep. There will be no dreaming tonight.

February 12, 2006
On the ceiling I see vultures swarming. There is a phone in my hand. With it, I attempt to call someone. The words sound frantic, desperate.

My heart beats on panic, not on blood or oxygen.

Maybe this phone call is too late.

The vultures above become ghosts and cloud-shaped figures.

February 14, 2006
Around my neck is a necklace. A heart-shaped pendant to remind me that I need to love myself.

February 25, 2006
Standing on a steep and icy slope, I slip and fall. Inside these walls, a week goes by. I am alone and destroy myself.

Food is impossible to swallow. Water will kill me. I still don't shower. Denton doesn't seem to notice my rough shape. No one does.

February 26, 2006

I pop a Red Rocket and chase it with a gulp of beer. In my pocket is some cocaine because I am too scared to leave the house without any. I am going to visit my aunt.

At the kitchen table she pours tea and I try to explain the contract work I am doing. But I want to be talking about the things we're not talking about.

I excuse myself to the washroom. In the mirror I see someone I don't know. Someone who is terrified. Someone who can't continue. This stranger reaches into my pocket and palms the baggie of cocaine. My hand is shaking. This shaking hand turns on the tap and lets water run inside the baggie. With my foot I open the small metal garbage can beside the sink and drop everything inside.

Back at Denton's I receive an email. My aunt does not want me back at her house for tea.

*

February 28, 2006

People do not understand why I am in the position that I am in because I try to project someone in a better environment.

Without explanation, I need to go to rehab.

March 1, 2006

I'm walking into an empty field. My purse lowers to the grass and the dogs hop out. I have two dogs now. Sisters. Sushi and Sashimi. They begin to prance and chase one another. Happy, fluffy, untroubled show girls. The air, warm from a Chinook, gives my face a hint of colour. There is hope in these dogs and in these days. There is hope in this moment. I stand here and hold onto it for all it's worth.

March 3, 2006

Throughout the nightclub his evil eye is following me. I do not want to fight. But his eye does not want me standing too close to anyone else. It does not want me to dance. But I must dance. So I do. And I am met with a hard shove. To the floor. My drink spills but I hold onto all emotions. My girlfriends look down at me and I remain calm.

I sneak out. After a long bus ride to nowhere my parents agree to put their credit card down at a motel. Somehow, I end up on a plane. Once again. To see what my past looks like.

Because the past can offer clues.

March 4, 2006

No matter where you run, there you are. It's not Denton and it's not drugs that I am running from. But myself. Around me, it's beautiful and rejuvenating to be away. But I am infected with this parasite. Moving beyond the past is an important step to living in the present.

Across from me, Lana picks up the phone and takes a stand against Denton. Lana is strong and in touch with herself. Right now I am the opposite. Watching her magnifies this. I want to hold it together. But I can't. So, after Lana hangs up the phone, I wait. Then call Denton myself to tell him I will be retuning the next day. It's not that I want to return to him. I just want to return to my reality. The one I cannot solve by running away.

To live in the past is to live depressed.

March 5, 2006

A documentary on rehab is playing. I watch it. I see people who have problems receive treatment. I see myself. At the end of the program, I learn that five of the six people have relapsed.

Right now I am sober from cocaine. But not sober of coffee, caffeine pills and ephedrine.

March 6, 2006

I throw up. Food exits my stomach and gives me temporary relief. But I am not done. So I pick at my face and destroy it. I am red and bleeding. Then I spend three hours cutting split ends individually off strands of hair.

I manage one breath.

The air comes into the top part of my lungs. Shallow. Further stimulating my sense of panic.

March 7, 2006

An ad campaign for the Heart and Stroke Foundation says that heart disease is the number one killer of women.

March 8, 2006

I've finished the last bottles of caffeine pills and ephedrine. They are empty. But I am full. Full of hatred, contempt, and anger. I want to kill Denton. If he touches me ever again I will kill him. To know myself capable of killing is new. And calming.

*

March 11, 2006

Denton and I fly to San José, Costa Rica. As we check into the hotel his eyes are glazed over and his mouth is twisted into a gnarl. He tosses one hundred dollars and his green backpack onto the hotel bed and leaves, slamming the door.

Part of me hopes he doesn't come back.

March 13, 2006

A shuttle bus lumbers towards a small town at the base of a volcano. All that is required of me is to put one foot in front of the other. The view at the top makes these uphill hikes worthwhile. I feel as alive as I thought I would. There is a waterfall. I swim. Tonight, a spa. Sitting in stones surrounded by tropical flowers and cascades of natural hot springs cleanses my spirit. In a sulphur mist, I blend into the landscape. Glistening, on the surface, my eyes match the sequins on this bikini.

Underneath it all, the shimmer graduates to a darker shade. Black, inky, poisonous. A hatred directed towards Denton. It wants to injure his ugliness. These thoughts are kept silent because in my version of rehab, this trip, there's no point of malice.

Unfortunately, I am not here on a personal mission. Denton kneels in front of me, and proposes that we get married. An absurd notion. The response is firm.

No.

As a matter of fact, I want to break up. For good.

March 14, 2006

To live in the hope of the future, I must stay in constant motion to accelerate getting there. This is non-stop. San José to La Fortuna by taxi. Then to Santa Elena by boat, horseback, and jeep. Then to Puntarenas by local bus. I buy sunglasses. Darker and larger than the previous pair.

With an entire face shielded like midnight, I feel safe from everything and everybody. Safe from alcohol. Even safe from

Denton. I'm hiding from the latter inside a cabana. He and cocaine find me by 3 am.

Evidently, I need more than sunglasses for protection.

I need to change my company.

March 15, 2006

A speedboat ploughs across the ocean, taking us to a surf town called Jaco. A lot of things are left behind. The task at hand is to kayak from the shore into menacing waves and a rock island where sharks graze. I should be a little sacred. Pound for pound their pointed fins sell for more than anything else in this part of the world. The rooftops further south are lined with shark fins drying in the sky. Painting the coast blood red. I close my eyes and land my kayak. Later, the narrow highways and small fishing villages become my personal expressway. We leave on a motorcycle. I experience real speed and relax. Exhaling for what feels like the first time.

March 19, 2006

This is my first time on the Caribbean coast. And it will not be my last. Love lives in the air and sand of Puerto Viejo and I am an observer to it. Not a participant.

Denton is demanding that we go out tonight. My strategy of avoiding the dark, him, and alcohol isn't sure about the challenge.

Inside a small and sweaty club the world seems at peace. Tanned and beautiful people vibrate. We dance as if one. In the distance the roaring waves crash against the Salsa Brava. Under the low ceiling, in thick air, against my back, I feel someone. Like magnets, we connect. The whole room is dancing. Swaying. Incoming and retreating. The whole world oscillates. Except Denton.

He grabs me by the triceps and rips me from the room. From the figure behind me. From the magnetism. Inside the rental car, with the gas pedal leveraged, we speed through the blackness of the night. Racing to the final showdown.

A head-on collision is not my concern. Nor is Denton's hand, gripped tightly around my neck. The air squeezes out from my throat and my eyes begin to bulge and water. Blood accumulates in the round parts of my face. I want him to keep squeezing. My contempt challenges him to crush my pharynx.

But he lets go.

We're still speeding. I can't see anything anymore. Blinded. It appears I will never again be the same.

It dawns on me that if I had a knife I would stab Denton. And never again stab myself.

We may not be able to avoid other people who inflict hurt. Other people's actions are out of our control. But for our own actions and feelings, we are responsible.

23

‖‖‖ ‖‖‖ ‖‖‖ ‖‖‖ ‖‖

"The good people I used to know
cannot seem to forgive what I've become."

April 20, 2006

Despite Denton's attempted sabotage I got back to Calgary and found someone willing to take me as a tenant. I am going to move out of Denton's. A character house, separated into four suites, will soon be home. Upstairs, downstairs, and beyond a partition wall are three other men. Other tenants. Security in the form of neighbours.

The landlord is handing me keys. The neighbour in the house to the east is watching. It appears that she feels a strong reaction to my arrival. She thinks that I am in danger.

With a poker face I respond casually and say that I work in sports advertising. That I paint. And run. By saying these things, I convince the interlocutors and become normal. And safe.

May 2, 2006

I enlisted my parents to travel 1,420 kilometres to help with the covert mid-day move.

May 3, 2006

Slipping into depression is the same as being trapped under concrete rubble in the aftermath of an earthquake. My parents take the dogs up north for safekeeping. Left here alone, I have no reason to function. No reason to eat. So I wait. On the floor.

There's peace in this position. And also tragedy. I fantasize about death. Not because I am going to act out any of these fantasies but because I don't have another outlet for the real pain living inside me. Only walls and windows separate it from the outside world.

May 10, 2006

Unaware of my emotional baggage, an office manager took me under her wing. I now play receptionist three days a week. Listening in, it's obvious that I need more instruction on how to answer a phone. Luckily, I'm friendly and a quick learner.

Gradually, the distance between the black hole at home and the light of the rest of the world shrinks. Enough, at least, to allow in some light. Some awareness. From a safe distance, I can enter a phase of observation.

May 17, 2006

To find someone who's willing to hold more than my hand will be hard. Alone still, my mind takes long runs along the Bow River. It moves much faster than my feet. It scurries so far away that I can't keep up.

June 17, 2006

Since I'm a receptionist so few days per week, I have time to try and socialise. The best method seems to be in what is called the gig economy. A company or agency hires me to represent a particular product at an event. Often I get to keep the outfit. While representing for Bacardi rum, I meet someone named Travis. He makes me laugh. We go for lunch at the most beautiful outdoor terrace. Then shopping. I learn that he is also in the middle of a transition. His most recent wife, number three, left him. And also, she took the dog.

Travis is sixty. In him I see that heartbreak is ageless. Transitions in life are ageless. Having the right attitude and perseverance is key. There is no better shelter for the lonely than in the company of another. Travis has become my best friend.

July 2, 2006

He pulls up in his cherry red Acura NSX. Impeccably dressed. I love this about Travis. His sense of style. He has other cars. Newer ones. But the NSX is my favourite.

With Travis I am re-learning the basis of friendship. A healthy friendship. Pure and simple. Attention, sharing, and not based on contingency.

July 8, 2006

Giddy up. The annual, raging, country western theme party known as Stampede is descending on Calgary. Wearing denim shorts that could be shared with a young child and carrying rope and guns, my cowgirl boots stomp the earth. Care of a one-thousand-dollar bribe that Denton paid me to continue not participating in his ongoing Assault charge trial, I have enough tequila to rival a small Mexican distillery.

I don't feel guilty for accepting a cash bribe from Denton. The police left the witness's name and phone number on the top of the relevant disclosure papers. The witness is no longer participating either. Just another of the innumerable flaws in the justice system, along with the prolonged hearings and general ineffectiveness.

August 1, 2006

I hadn't planned to see Denton. Then he walked into my office and stole my bike. I want to ignore him, but I also want my bike back.

August 28, 2006

In the staff kitchen, I open a bottle of antihistamines and consume the contents. Sedated, I look to be passed out at my desk. Actually, I'm hanging in there.

No one seems to notice.

October 2, 2006

It's becoming evident why I like Travis and my neighbours so much. I feel safe around them. I want to feel safe. I want to feel safe inside myself.

October 19, 2006

At work, I'm looking at bikini-clad celebrities on the Internet when a man comes in to serve me. The paperwork indicates that I am being sued. For custody of the dogs.

Subsequent investigation reveals that Denton has been harassing the breeder who sold them to me. He has forged a Bill of Sale to the Canadian Kennel Club, naming himself as the new owner.

It looks like I have no choice but to play ball with the legal system. In a dog-custody lawsuit.

October 22, 2006

At my latest gig, selling designer vacuums, I am not entertained. Homer's philosophy is off. In youth and beauty wisdom is not rare, it's just that nobody stopped to ask.

Department stores, deep in the suburbs, are boring. Just as I decide to hide in the washroom to eat dried blueberries from a Ziploc bag, my phone rings. It's a lawyer.

She's going to help me for free. Her first advice is that I write an affidavit. A personal decree of the truth of certain statements or claims.

This could be war.

The problem with war, I find, is that there is no such thing as an external enemy. But my lawyer assures me that there's no room for philosophy in court. Instead, she wants a concise timeline of the horror show known as my ex-boyfriend.

At this point, I'm open to the idea of a restraining order, minus the fact that Denton is who gave me a ride to my current location in the suburbs.

It turns out I am still human. Sometimes, he is too.

October 23, 2006

Since I am scared of men it makes sense to experiment with women. The novelty of this may work. Also, the sense of safety. Even though there is no safe haven from abuse, that small fact isn't on my mind.

My next lover will be sexy and blonde. And female.

November 3, 2006

My lawyer made it very clear that I must stop using Denton as a chauffeur and brave the elements. Which equates to minus twenty-two degrees and windy. To work with the law, I must stop being human.

The bitter cold makes me think even more about death. About jumping off the Crowchild overpass into oncoming traffic or flinging myself into the river's weir. If I was dead, the cold would stop. I write to my grandma. She responds with a full-length mink coat. Luckily, curled up inside mink, I am warm and, possibly, no longer sad.

*

November 10, 2006

I wish it wasn't true that I met my girlfriend in Denton's bed.

81

But sometimes wishing can be futile. She was in it, naked. With him. I shouldn't have been over there in the first place, but nagging loneliness can compel bad decisions. Seeing them broke my already-shattered insides into tinier, sharper pieces. Alas, no one will hear me cry over it because she left him. To be with me.

This isn't a conventional way to start a relationship. Blurring the lines between a friend and an enemy. Though as someone who's definition of Love and Hate are just as blurred, I don't mind. Maybe this is the real mechanism of war, to keep your enemies close.

Either that or I'm simply working within the prevailing circumstances.

Selene, my new girlfriend, is blonde and sexy and confident.

December 18, 2006
The job of a mirror is to show us how we look. But it reflects, in reality, an image that is significantly altered. It is always backwards.

Selene, it turns out, is my mirror image.

December 20, 2006
Love-hate relationships. I enter into these externally because this is what I'm used to with myself. My promise to the lawyer and to Selene and to countless other people is once again broken because I let Denton into my house. It did not go well. Spotting photographs of me with Selene, he attacked. I finally accept that I create my problems by opening the door to them. Ushering them in. Maybe I enjoy flirting with fire. But sometimes it only leaves me burnt.

Research shows that a lot of people are stuck in a love-hate relationship. We love something. But also hate it. To learn about this one must understand that self-sabotage is never intended to be negative. The intent is always positive. Whether that's smoking, eating too much junk food, or holding onto someone who hits us. The intent of our actions is never to sabotage. But, regardless, our self becomes inescapably damaged.

This is why I'm stuck. Being with Denton can be less terrifying than being alone. And fear is a powerful emotion. I know this because it is exactly what prevents me from shutting the door on this terrible cycle. Once and for all.

December 23, 2006
The outward me wants a hug. The inward me, the infinite me, also wants a hug. Simple emotional reinforcement. Back in my hometown for the Christmas holidays, my childhood sweetheart seems like a safe bet for this embrace. Unfortunately, but not unsurprisingly, I am wrong.

He does not want to hug me. Instead he tells me how shitty I am. That he's in a new relationship. And that he has learned, from time apart, how worthless our past together was.

These are things I don't need to hear. Words that feel like a dagger, thrust straight into my chest, twisted cautiously, and retracted in a neat and precise effort. The usual security I have in his presence is gone. It feels like a death. Like something I need to mourn. I don't think I have any real friends anymore. The good people I used to know cannot seem to forgive what I've become.

*

January 7, 2007
A new year poses an opportunity to leave last year's problems behind.

But Denton, someone I'm legally and morally supposed to stay away from, seems to be the only person flying me to

83

tropical islands. So that's that then. I'll have to ask my lawyer if breaching the restraining order counts if vacationing to the Dominican Republic.

Travel can offer more than rehab. It can open your eyes to the world at large. With just a plane ride's distance everything washes away in the tropics. Even though the seashells seem to lack in abundance, the length and texture of the local women's hair doesn't. It's the most beautiful hair I have ever seen. These women are gorgeous. An attitude, I note, that proves I'm not totally bitter or irreversibly ruined.

One day, I want to feel beautiful too. Until then, I prefer incognito. Hidden, I watch a boy who's selling horseback rides along the beach. I don't want to ride one of the horses but to know where he comes from. I emerge to ask him to take us to his village. To a typical disco. He agrees.

Getting away from the tourists, the resort, and the all-inclusive formula feels freeing. Happiness, here, is a pink hat to match pink shoes. Entire families of five pile onto a scooter for an evening out. Here, I think I have smiled.

After the success of the village excursion, we abandon the resort altogether and rent a car. We drive through endless sugar cane fields. The only interruption in the landscape is a snack cart. On seeing it I realise that I'm hungry. Several muscular and shirtless men wait in line. Field workers. Entering the line-up, they look at me curiously. When it's my turn I load up on sweetened peanuts for the journey.

Eventually we arrive at Boca Chica. I'm wading past a soccer game, through shallow water to a sandbar. In infinite turquoise ocean I learn that I can choose to be weak, or I can choose to be strong. There is the capacity for both.

A European man in a tiny Speedo wades beside me. I stare at his swimwear. It reveals tan lines and a giant bulge.

22

"There is no crying in jail."

January 11, 2007

I've been studying to become a professional. A professional Real Estate Agent. The last session of required training is complete, the test is passed, and the fees are paid. I am officially a Real Estate Agent, licensed to buy and sell houses on behalf of clients.

January 17, 2007

In front of me is a married man. He is old, short, perky in personality, and arrogant. He is hitting on me. In an alcohol-induced moment, he quips that I shouldn't care about his marriage. The truth is, even though the concept of marriage is abstract, I do care. Mostly because the concept of cheating is crystal clear.

Leaving someone completely for another lover is fine. It's intermittent lying that's problematic. The notion that his actions have the power to hurt another is foreign to this man.

Aside from the fact that his physical attributes are less than alluring, the last thing I need is to be discovered by his wife. She could be a jealous type.

Naturally, I have come to know firsthand that jealous lovers are crazy.

He persists, pressing his presidential-status-claiming business card into my hand. Though this might be how to build a Rolodex of future clients. It's tough to do business with men

85

who are blatantly trying to sleep with you, but not impossible. Nothing in Real Estate is impossible. Just like in Life, in Real Estate, anything is possible.

For the right price.

*

January 22, 2007

Being in and out of court has taught me that lawyers have a seriously dry, red-tape laden, tedious, aesthetically non-stimulating, and sterile atmosphere in which to work.

I listen in on a discussion between two attorneys and one judge. A case where some ex-lawyer is challenging his disbarment. Their conclusion is to re-adjourn to set the time for setting the time of a judicial review on setting the time.

I decide to leave the claustrophobically wood-panelled room for some air.

January 23, 2007

The timing of major events often dictates their success or failure. We can only deal with things in whichever way we are capable of at the given time. There's no rewind button, pause button, or other magical power to optimize timing.

Again in court, I go over details of the restraining order request that my lawyer is processing. It is accepted by the Court of Queen's Bench, by some Honourable Judge, without question. But it's simply much too late to be of service.

Some people believe in the saying, better late than never. The jury happens to be out regarding its validity.

January 31, 2007

Whether legal restraint is a solution to violence, I don't know.

86

Apparently it will clear the air on who owns which dogs. Otherwise, domestic violence is a complicated affair. People, who know my situation from the outside, affirm that the helplessness has been very real. People say that if things escalate the police can now react meaningfully. This is what they tell me. But this is not how the world actually works.

In reality my custody hearing may be in a year. A timeline I cannot endure. Denton stalks me. In my nightmares and in broad daylight.

In the meantime, those around me are like the villagers in Aesop's fable. The one with the boy and the wolf and the fictitious crying.

For some, sight of a predator might cause audible screams. Others might be scared into silence. Do you scream when a predator isn't present? This negative attention may be worth playing pretend for. But I am not pretending. My life is terrorised by this dangerous animal. So what are the other options? To learn how to coax it. To learn how to feed it enough whilst determining a safe distance. I will not be the boy who cried wolf. Instead, I will become a wolf tamer.

February 21, 2007

I should be trying to hunt for clients. Instead, Selene and I are bored with one another alone and seek entertainment. The distinction between working and partying is a learning curve. One that is challenging for someone like me to decipher considering the abundance of social attention present during both.

March 8, 2007

I continue to go out and continue to meet innumerable people. There is the possibility that I can help some of them with property. However, no one captures me. No one holds my being suspended in the realm of bliss that I crave. In general, most people have nothing to offer.

However, being safe from external stimuli of the having-a-crush variety is good because, every day, I swing wildly between a state of devastation and tears to one of anger and resentment. Any more turbulence would be catastrophic.

To protect the unsuspecting general public from myself, a disaster, I refuse to discuss publicly the topic of emotional turbulence. I lock all my emotions away. Into hiding. This, I call the vault.

*

March 16, 2007
Denton slashed my tires. Denton then paid for new tires. Then he broke into my yard and stole the dogs.

Flabbergasted, I called the police. Who tell me that retrieving anything from inside his personal property falls outside of their jurisdiction.

There's been a time when an officer drove to Denton's house and escorted me inside. That was then and this is now. The inconsistency is outrageous. But I understand the brutal, unfair truth. Court dates, as I know, take forever. Lawyers are expensive. Police are limited actors. And the law of possession states that he or she in possession has the upper hand.

March 22, 2007
I've had enough. Or I've had too much. The war is coming.

I will reclaim my dogs.

March 23, 2007
My cell phone dials 911. I state an address and warning. That shit's about to go down.

Calling the police on yourself is a big mistake. Obviously not something I took the time to think about. As my car slows to park in front of Denton's, my only thought is that I want my dogs and I want them now. Repetition to the sound of a drum.

I remove my blazer and unbutton the striped oxford shirt underneath. Brown leather boots pulled atop designer skinny jeans gleam in the sunlight. The better part of my outfit, a gift from Travis, looks fantastic.

Mentally, the forecast is ugly.

The drum beats louder.

I approach the front door and swiftly kick in the lower glass-detailed portion. Some of it shatters, some bends inwards. The dogs come running. Carefully, I grab them. With pooches cradled in-arm, I turn around to return to my car just as Denton and two police cruisers pull up.

I am no longer holding the fluffy animals but my own hands behind my back. Hard metal handcuffs cut into my skin. Ushered into the back seat of a cruiser, I try to break my hands to escape the cuffs. I try to no avail. The door closes.

Trapped, I start crying, screaming, and begging. I yell profanities. I yell about how unfair the legal system is. About how for a year everyone wanted to help me. How for a year I rejected help. I make it clear that these dogs are everything. Finally, I yell that I have an upcoming custody hearing and a restraining order against Denton.

Even though I clearly drove here, after contemplating this last point the officer leaves the car and has his colleague arrest Denton into the other vehicle.

The officer returns to the driver's seat. Through the security barrier I'm being told that my name is associated with a file. A file either explains things or makes them more confusing. He doesn't elaborate. We drive to a parking lot beside an elementary school. He parks the car and turns to look at me through the bullet-proof wall that separates the back seat from him and his electronics in the front.

He begins to talk.

This is not protocol, this is counselling.

He tells me that I am beautiful. That I have things to look forward to. That I should have nothing to do with a man like Denton.

I stop thrashing and the panic stops. These are things I need to hear. However, the timing and circumstance surrounding his delivery is bad. It's worse than bad. I am handcuffed in the backseat of a police cruiser and cannot hold onto a single thing this man is telling me.

My mind resumes the maniacal rampage. Thunderbolts and lightening.

He restarts the car.

I hear screaming.

It's coming from me.

I'm going to jail.

*

March 24, 2007

Jail was a dehumanizing experience. And also one of the best things to ever happen to me. After arriving, there were some necessary logistics. My personal items were confiscated, including the leather boots.

I am told that these are evidence of the crime scene.

Inside a cell, I am placed with two other women. The fat one tells me the basic protocol.

There is no crying in jail.

The one who is strung out on methamphetamines has been here for hours. Something to do with a stolen car. The fat one is

90

here for passing out inside a house that wasn't hers to be drunk inside. Beside these two, I sit. The conversation serves me well. Then, the conversation stops and I start to panic.

Why am I still here?

I learn that as a first-time offender I will be released. I want to know when. One of the jail mates, the fat one, has priors. She is being sent to Remand in the morning. To do real jail time. I have no idea what this means. I learn that she is pregnant. Not fat. I learn that in real jail she won't be fed properly to sustain a healthy baby.

Before I can be sad about this, more women begin to join us in the cell.

Prostitutes. The homeless. Those from situations possibly more dire than my own. As the cell fills, I am no longer eligible for a spot on the bench. Standing at the door, I peer between the bars, wanting to be out of this hell. From the toilet, a woman with acne and bad polyester track pants produces a crack pipe from inside her body. Then, a lighter. I stand in horror and listen to her smoke crack by the toilet, three and a half meters behind me.

Holding onto the bars that are the door, staring into the hallway, I forget the cordial rule and start sobbing. In fact, wailing.

Under the salty tears, the skin on my face feels dry.

In the distance, Denton starts cooing my nickname. Birdie. I want to scream. My sobbing is interrupted by the swishing sound of cheap track pants chafing between fat thighs.

The track-pant-clad woman brings her face close enough for me to smell the odorous stench of crack cocaine and poor dental hygiene. She tells me to shut my mouth. Then asks if I want something else to cry about. Instinctively, I tell her to get the fuck away from me. She backhands me. Hard. My face stays turned to the side. Looking away.

She finishes by saying that she will put me in a grave. I don't doubt her ability.

Immediately my tears stop. My skin feels even drier. More fragile.

I eventually turn around and shut up. I do not need to get my ass kicked inside jail. I'm bewildered that no one comes to reprimand this woman for her behaviour. Inside the cell it's a free for all. Hence the no crying rule.

After finger printing and photos, I meet with the in-house lawyer on duty. In front of him, I am inconsolable. A nurse comes to give me a tranquilizer. Sedated, back in the cell, a space becomes available on the bench.

A cheese sandwich and a juice box arrive. After eating, I wait.

Finally, inside a white room with fluorescent lighting, a podium, and a microphone, someone is telling me why I am in jail. I have been here for twenty hours. The entire time Denton has been down the hall. Twenty hours feels like twenty years. My skin feels like the Sahara.

The detained men, from their separate cells, now know my nickname. They have been chanting it for hours. Taunting me.

Birdie.

Birdie.

Birdie.

This is what echoes down the hall behind me as I am permitted to leave.

They're keeping my boots. In exchange, I receive paperwork and my other affairs. I am facing charges of Breaking and Entering and Intent to Commit an Indictable Offense. Denton is facing the rest of his weekend in Remand. With all his priors, multiple Assault charges, Domestic Violence, and Kidnapping, to name a few, he requires a real judge. One who will not start work until Monday.

March 25, 2007

I call Travis. He's on a golf course. Laughing robustly at Calgary's newest species of jailbird. With no idea where the dogs are, I can ignore not having footwear. The fur babies remain an immediate priority. Back at my car, a note tucked under the windshield wiper reveals their whereabouts.

This is absolutely contrary to police protocol. By now, so is my entire situation.

The noted address is a home belonging to Denton's neighbour and friend. I knock on the door. It's answered to a percussion roll. The final performance. Threatening. Or quite pathetic.

I manage to procure the canines.

With possession being nine-tenths of the law, I have won.

The drumroll stops.

April 1, 2007

Underneath a chocolate brown sweater dress I flex my muscles as hard as I can. It's the only thing I can do to distract myself from how sick I feel. The room is chilly. Outside, even worse. My car is parked at the YMCA two blocks away from the Alberta Provincial Courthouse. I'm here for what they call a First Appearance.

My game plan is to request to adjourn the first appearance because I want legal counsel.

Outside the courtroom someone approaches me to ask how I'm doing. I explain my request. To my surprise, the response is that my charges may be getting dropped.

Now it's become a waiting game. I'm anxious. So I watch people. One of the lawyers looks Italian. His suit is beautiful and his glasses are made of ivory. Another, a curly haired beast of a man, looks 300 pounds. And Texan. His handlebar moustache and thick accent alone weigh more than me. He moves sporadically with flailing limbs and theatrical gestures. Like he's conducting a sermon to a group of radical religious zealots. I am glad neither of these men are my representation.

The people addressing the judge are typical. Woman beaters. Some Caucasian, some Middle Eastern. The only case that strikes me as interesting is a Swahili prisoner. His white eyes captivate against his midnight complexion. His interpreter is adorned in gold jewelry like he plans to film a rap video, not address a court. The judge is concerned about the accused's refusal to use legal aid. His intentions come across flawless to me. Fuck de lawyer, man. Lock him up. He did it, man. No need a lawyer.

The seriousness of my situation suddenly pales in comparison. Breaking and Entering. Attempt to Commit an Indictable Offence. I do not feel like a criminal and I do not belong in this room.

I try to think about how I got here. A year ago I sat in another room with employees from Home Safe and the Victim Assistance Program. Back then I was, according to these people, a victim. I can tell that now I am different. Not quite the opposite, but somewhere in between. Someone whose entire future hinges on having a clean criminal record. It is not permissible to sell homes if I am convicted of B and E.

I'm starting to feel sorry for myself but then my name is called. Eyes wide open, I stand and walk to the front of the room. The Crown Prosecutor enters to discuss my case with the Judge for the second time. This man I recognise as Denton's lawyer from last year.

My legs are shaking. I don't know if they will hold me. Then I hear. Crystal clear. The charges are dropped. I am free with no consequence. I manage a meek thank you. And leave.

How anticlimactic.

How perfect.

2 I

||||| ||||| ||||| ||||| |||

"Misery loves company."

April 3, 2007

Selene tells me that Botox and microdermabrasion can combat the stress I see on my face. After microdermabrasion left me with eczema, a red-rashy bandit, I decide to try Botox anyways.

There are numerous studies that show that the act of physically smiling can make you feel happy. I hope the converse is also true.

Some people call wrinkles worry lines. The nurse explains that Botox prevents the muscles from being able to contract. If my face can't make a worried expression, aspects of the emotion may stop. Worrying is like praying for what you don't want to happen.

In life, you must focus on what is happening, without worries. And one day, maybe, without Botox.

April 4, 2007

The thing about falling in love is that it also helps to rid distress. This isn't what I had in mind at tonight's grand opening. A renovated playhouse-cum-upscale-eatery-and-hockey-viewing-mega-club built in the 1920s. Turns out I need those newly in-love endorphins to lift my spirits.

Latching on to one of two flame-shaped handles, I swing open the front door and walk into a combination of ornate grandness juxtaposed with tacky merchandising. The walls are upholstered with aluminum, to look like ice, and red suede fabric.

Ascending the winding stairwell I reach an upper-level bar and viewing atrium. The overwhelming array of television screens that line the back wall of what was once a theatre, a massive fibre optic conglomerate, ceases to distract me from the guy Selene is drinking with at the bar below. Giant lights, angled peculiarly from the vast main-room ceiling, cast a red glow upon both of them.

Something about him tantalises me. Most probably the cornflower blue eyes, which somehow are not dulled by the distance nor the lights.

I drink my drink. Liquid courage.

Passing more siren red lighting, I exit through the side door. We're leaving. Not Selene and I. But me and blue eyes. His name is Robert. He's tall and sturdy and has the jawline of a Disney hero.

It's possible that there are hundreds of other guys in this club, and in the world for that matter. Selene can have all of them. Just not this one.

April 7, 2007

With Robert, who tells me he is the VP of a start-up technology company and works so hard that he seldom has time for a personal life, I try to keep the things in the vault to myself. Details about emotional swinging, jail, restraining orders, and rescinding the restraining orders. But, I also desperately need someone to talk to. To satisfy both wants, I half talk and I half hold back.

This is like standing on a dock beside a lake. There are two canoes. What you want and what you need. I enter both even though they're not travelling in the same direction. One foot's inside Canoe Want, the other stands in Canoe Need. Water pulls in opposite directions and it's only a matter of time before my balance falters to gravity and I capsize. Until this happens, I lie. To myself and to everyone around me.

This is called coping.

April 10, 2007

Selene, her luscious mouth, and a smiley Travis relax in the hot tub while I bask in sunshine on the balcony. An orange sunrise casts citrus hues onto the eastern cityscape and my own house far in the distance. An abode recently revealed to contain mice.

At Travis's there is no worry about vermin. There is no worry about anything. Lingering in the air, the smell of barbequed turkey and apple sausages. A feast we ate like it could be our last. The party is never ending. Smatterings of Gouda cheese, crackers, fudge cake brownies, empty bottles of wine, and an array of tequila serves as evidence. Travis's maid will be in shortly to clean everything up.

Misery loves company. Most people forget this. I prefer company as far opposite to miserable as possible. Luminous. We vow to bask in the positive. Sunrise brunch. Al fresco. The fresh air is perfect. And then, one mouthful at a time, one laugh at a time, the smiles begin to add up. Smiles, it turns out, are bankable. You can draw on them in the future.

April 15, 2007

From my window, I can glance into my neighbour's house across the street. It's always bustling. He does some Yoga every day and has endless social companions. I am not yet interested in Yoga but am intrigued by my neighbour and his friends. Even though most of them are gay men, I eventually get asked out.

April 16, 2007

He pours and stamps concrete for a living. He drives a motorcycle. Sitting on the back is to trust the driver. To trust the road. To trust the universe.

The date was going well until he decided to tell me how great I'd be pregnant. A strange comment. It renders intense paranoia. Like slang for being called fat. I absolutely hate my little round tummy pooch.

April 21, 2007

Sometime between 2 pm and 5 pm my house got burgled.

Among the items stolen, listed in a Calgary Police document titled *Appendix A: Items Stolen* are five pairs of stilettos, fluorescent green running shoes, two dogs, two dog leashes, a spare key, a black leather bomber jacket, a red wool dress coat, and a two-inch flat iron for hair straitening.

I expected random uniformed officers to attend the call. However, both of them claim to know me. This is not to my advantage. One of them scolds me not to contact Denton under any circumstance, and the other poorly hides his childish amusement. Blinded by thick smoke, I see nothing humorous.

My house is on fire and I'm burning. Adrenalin carries me to the river beyond the backyard just as embers scald my skin.

I'm blistering.

At the river's edge, my reflection showcases a roughened, soot-covered face. The cold river water can quench this dry, parched, and tense mouth. But the refreshing water is out of reach. If I had one of the stilettos, things would be different. I would be taller. I could reach. Crumbling instead, low to the ground, the fire continues to burn. I fall to ashes.

April 23, 2007

It's nothing new for Selene to pick up some guy from the bar. This one just-so-happens to be storing my things, excluding the dogs, at his house. I have no idea why he confessed this to her.

Harbouring stolen goods of such irrelevance to any male in his mid-thirties is pathetic. It turns out that this man is a coke head. Someone I knew in the past.

Instead of calling the police ever again, I call the addict's alleged girlfriend to ask her permission to drive myself to an address in SW Calgary to her boyfriend's house. I do not seek any kind of scene or wish to engage in any sort of dialogue. His girlfriend can choose whether to agree to this based on her interpretation of what is going on. She is speechless.

Wearing a wrinkled black trench, not my standard red garment of the moment, and with frizzy hair, the direct result of the break-in, I hope this guy, seeing me in disarray, feels guilty for his involvement. And this man is guilty. He is standing in front of me crying.

His pain makes me stand taller with poise. I am here to reclaim footwear. The stilettos, back on my feet, look fabulous.

*

April 26, 2007

Since the most recent robbery I've been commiserating with alcohol. Drunk, I shouldn't be driving but like to play roulette.

In theory, if I can physically make it into the car, I am fit to drive.

I dial Robert and try not to be too dramatic. The tears are not in anger but because I am alone. The killer black-resin platform heels that seemed so important actually give me nothing. I wish

99

I was with Robert, being held in his strong, stable embrace, and I miss the dogs, and I have no idea how to get him to want to hang out, nor how to get the dogs back. Lawfully.

Driving recklessly, I don't hide how wasted I am. Calling attention to myself, the police or whoever else sees me can laugh or lecture all they want. This foot to the pedal will not relent. Not for traffic lights, not for anything.

April 27, 2007
It looks like Robert didn't call back. Knowing that I'm a liar, a frequent drunken mess, and disgusting, he probably never will.

May 1, 2007
I spent every dollar I have on new clothes. In them, at some ice hockey playoff game, I feel sexy. Until I confront the ashamed person who is too scared to be seen as-is underneath, I will be a well-costumed fake.

May 3, 2007
Visiting Calgary, my parents want to meet for dinner. This seems too challenging. I tell myself how they aren't in my movie script right now. Life as a movie, our only power is to decide who is and who is not in the screenplay. The plot is to forget about the purloined pets and forget about Robert. Parents don't seem likely to assist in this, so instead I cast an unknown from an online dating site.

He pulls up in a convertible. Silver, but not an Audi. His first statement, as he stares with derision at my four-inch high heels, is that I should change into some flip-flops. I laugh as if this is a hilarious suggestion.

For the insecure, the same trait in another is intolerable. I decide I want to torture this man. I don't change shoes. We set off to order cocktails, beer, and weird combination shooters. Not because he isn't taking me for dinner. But because I can't eat in front of strangers.

My restlessness grows severe. Agitated, I cannot sit still. So I stand. Something is fundamentally wrong with this man's personality. I want to punch him in the face. So I stare him down ferociously and demand that he tells me how disgusting I am. If he doesn't obey quickly with a suitably insulting statement, I'm going to make him.

By connecting my fist with his gut.

He seems to find me charming. He finds the frustration cute and begins grabbing my chin and pinching my cheek. Laughing and smiling.

End scene.

Perhaps dining with my parents would have been a better option.

May 5, 2007

My car has been keyed. A metal line extends from the driver side door, down the side, across the rear bumper, and around back up the other side.

The chipped paint path leads to four letters staring at me. SLUT.

May 7, 2007

Sexiness is a personality trait. It seems to be the only personality trait other people around me associate with confidence. Since my confidence is low, I try to compensate through provocation.

Then, get drunk.

May 20, 2007

Barfing I can handle. Being wasted helps me pass out. Passing out helps me sleep.

Whether or not my entourage understands why I'm boozing, I don't know. We're on a camping trip. Some drug called MDMA is circulating the grounds. Through a campfire it doesn't matter who is high and who is not. Notably, I have not taken any.

The licking red flames illuminate a dog. There's smoke in my eyes. I am sad and I am alone and I see this dog. And I want to kill somebody. I want my own dogs to be here at the party.

I turn to the right to demand the bottle of whatever the person beside me has in hand. I don't need to be conscious. Slamming as much as I can stomach, I make my way to the back of someone's truck.

Blackness doesn't come. Instead, rage. It can't be killed with alcohol. Not even whisky.

Tearing off my own clothes, no one restrains me. Kicking and screaming, I exit the truck. Bare feet in soft earth. I remember falling down. Flailing, like a psychotic. I remember throwing up. I remember everything.

Everything that I so desperately want to forget.

May 21, 2007

The sun comes up. Various bruises from last night's episode are starting to show. Someone, awake at the picnic table, recounts how hilarious I looked tumbling down the hill backwards. He is amazed that I am not seriously injured.

It's freezing. All I can muster to announce is how intolerably cold it is. This is likely due to the fact that I'm not wearing any trousers. Being pants-less is funny. So I laugh.

Selene is not laughing. She is concerned about my behaviour. I embarrass her. I respond by calling her things that don't need to be repeated. I call her everything that would kill me to hear about myself. I'm sure everyone within a five-kilometre radius, if they weren't aware before, now knows that I'm not OK. I'm fucking crazy.

They're all on drugs yet, somehow, I'm the one who's not lucid.

*

May 22, 2007

Someone's feeding me South African giant prawns. Food like this has an immediate therapeutic effect. The chef's friend, a lawyer, specialises in real estate conveyancing. He tells me that if I put myself to work as a Real Estate Agent, I can do well for myself.

By telling me this he isn't going to save the world. But by telling me this he is going to save me. In charity there is an expression about a hand-out versus a long-term solution. Giving someone food is a good one-time act. Encouraging someone to her new vocation will help with feeding for many nights to come.

I leave to lie under a tree on a bed of moss and begin to consider the notion of work. The sun makes teasing appearances above my body. I relax.

I can do this. I can get it together.

*

June 1, 2007

It turns out that longing has addictive qualities. Scientifically, this is proven. I can tell it's true because I continue to long for someone. Specifically, for Robert. Handsome, hard-working Robert. As an emotion, longing is better than anger. But also depressing. As recourse, I investigate an alternative. Robert's lookalike. Someone named Jeremy.

The rivalry between him and Selene was immediate. Inevitable when alpha dominant personalities clash. This led to a dramatic exit by Selene and space for me to properly assess this Jeremy fellow. He started by announcing how he is aware, from friends, that I have serious problems.

I can't deny these allegations and no amount of vodka is going to mask the degree of truth to his claims. Good timing for a suggestion to go back to his condo and smoke something.

Crushing a Red Bull can, I make a bowl then use my earring to create holes in the aluminum. A can pipe. Unfortunately, marijuana does not help to calm me. Instead, like usual, paranoia prevails.

Jeremy's friends are telling me stories about his nickname. Scorpion. An animal that decapitates its mate. How lovely.

In the living room are fluorescent panties, presumably left by the stripper hired to dance here earlier on. Jeremy starts to undress me while his friends continue to point out various scorpion-embellished paraphernalia decorating the apartment. By now I'm feeling uncomfortable.

We make our way towards the master bedroom while he begins to undress himself. Experiencing the scorpion seems a bad idea. It seems I'm actually terrified of any man who isn't Robert. No matter how close the stunt double.

Jeremy goes into the washroom and I grab my things. Closer than the front door is a patio leading to a secure upper-level terrace. I'm climbing and trying to make an exit. Knocking on several neighbouring sliding glass doors proves unsuccessful. With no other option, I begin to scale down the lattice and fence, then jump onto street level.

June 2, 2007

Five large bags of Hawkins Cheezies are my console. I eat them all. This is my new thing. Eating my emotions.

In my pocket is a hipflask of Crown Royal. It's broad daylight and I'm going to whichever bar I end up in.

Standing in a narrow breezeway between the bar and the bar's washroom facility, I drop my phone. It breaks.

A broken phone correlates with a broken me.

This is my second phone this month. The one previous I voluntarily decided to smash into the pavement. Mostly to make it difficult to drunk dial Robert.

The plastic casing separates from the electronic innards. Green and metallic colours sparkle against the asphalt. A mosaic of momentary relief. I can't afford new phones but it's worth it. Breaking something.

Haziness is settling in the air. The transition between day and night.

My face is wet with tears and I can't find my car. I don't remember where it is and take a cab home to fetch my purple Norco mountain bike. Inside a portable coffee cup, I pour some dark rum. It's night and I'm wearing sunglasses and am, in any case, inebriated blind. I pedal along the pathways that wind past the Saddledome along the river. I keep pedalling under a bridge then across McLeod Trail. With each turn I lean as far as I can.

I want to crash. Eventually, I fall. Lying underneath the bike on a bed of grass in the lawn of some condo building, I rest. Part of me hopes that someone will think I've been hit. That I've been in an accident. And in some ways I have.

I want a stranger to attend the scene. No one comes. I open my eyes and try to look around. I'm not lying helpless in the grass. I'm in sky-high heels standing inside the basement of a club.

Someone is asking me what I want to drink.

Scotch. On the rocks.

20

IIII IIII IIII IIII IIII

"Many answers are revealed by the questions we ask."

July 10, 2007

Things have a way of working out when you need them to the most.

To handle and negotiate large sums of money is odd because I do not have any money of my own. A fact that I keep hidden. Except from Selene. She knows exactly how broke I am. She doesn't have much either.

My landlord emails me to say that he can no longer support my situation. I have not paid rent in two months. Thankfully, I can respond and say that I have the money to pay him back. Which I do, because I sold my first property.

The client let me take him to absolutely everything available in several neighbourhoods so that I could learn the market. Among these properties he found a place that he liked. I wrote the contract and negotiated the terms of the sale.

To celebrate I am hosting a party with Selene. Concurrently, Calgary's annual country western festival is starting. Stampede.

This year we all have something to celebrate.

July 14, 2007

Out and about, men approach. This isn't new. But the topic of conversation is. They are outright offering me money. Not to work as a Real Estate Agent. Just to have sex.

One's first encounter with prostitution is somewhat disgusting. So, I leave the propositions behind. Partially because I still just want to be with Robert, but also because I have found a satisfactory cowboy replacement who I don't want to run away from. Someone my age and innocent. Money can buy anything except moments like these. We are enchanted with one another and wild and free. We're on my purple mountain bike. Doubling home.

Save a horse. Ride a bike. And your cowboy.

July 23, 2007

A man standing in front of our matching black and white gingham shirts is asking Travis if I have a twin sister. An evil twin. I don't acknowledge him but Travis confirms in chuckle, I am the evil twin. Our plastic party glasses, full of fruit puree mixed with vodka, agree.

The evil twin, an antagonist found in many different fictional genres, is a physical copy of the protagonist. With a radically inverted morality.

I wonder about the man who's asking. Many answers are revealed by the questions we ask.

In later conversation, Travis discloses that the inquirer is a philanthropist. With fifty-something years to my twenty-four. Evil or pure, I am intrigued.

July 25, 2007

The local news shows a Mexican mariachi band. I'm singing along in the background. The front page of today's newspaper chronicles my dance moves.

At Salsa Fest, it seems I am the only one on the dancefloor at 11 am. Luckily, it feels good. Dancing with myself.

*

July 28, 2007

Travis has been divorced. Perhaps it isn't possible to remain happily married forever. People change as they get older. In life, two things are inevitable. One is that everybody dies. No one is immune to death. The other is that nothing is permanent. We must embrace impermanence.

The affluent men and women I meet lately all seem to be successfully divorced and moving onto second phases of being. According to Travis, I should start to formulate a game plan for myself. To carefully observe and decide where I want to be when I'm fifty. That through a combination of business strategy and marriage or dating, I can be good to myself. Versus what I have been in the past. Detrimental.

I listen but don't respond with the truth. That I want to follow my heart. But that my heart is broken.

Imagine following a broken GPS. Owning a compass that doesn't point north. The part about always letting your conscience be your guide seems to have failed. I think my ability to know right from wrong took a hike.

The remaining game plan is really simple. Be happy or die trying.

Since I don't have a partner, let alone a third spouse, I can't identify with everything that Travis says. But I deeply respect what he is trying to teach me about strategy. That if I put my mind to it, I can execute a game plan and get anything I want. It seems my back-up game plan, after happiness, is to have nice clothes.

August 3, 2007

In Miami at a swanky hotel along Ocean Avenue, I luxuriate. Coming here on a whirlwind to celebrate my birthday seemed a good idea. The other reality is someone struggling to formulate a game plan. Someone who wants to be free even though most people seem to think that freedom is something that money can pay for.

Miami is a good place to analyse these things. In its potpourri of multi-culturalism, acceptance lives. In my pocket, two dollars. My life savings at this point. All the more reason to stay at South Beach.

On my skin, coconut Vaseline oil. Slick, I slide across leather benches inside limousines and go from pool to lounge to nightclub, getting shinier as the night progresses.

I command twenty-two magnums of champagne to the VIP section. The bottles, gigantic, arrive in the arms of tiny girls in even tinier dresses. Sparklers alert the crowd below that those above are popping bottles. As each bottle arrives, I pass it on to whichever girl hovering close by looks like she deserves it.

My friends love the attention. One of them has the club management shut down the washroom so he can get some private time in with a handful of Babies. That's what he calls the girls around here. Me, I'm the Princess.

Instead of drinking, her highness sneaks out past crowds of people into the street. For some reason, for once, I'm sober.

Back at the hotel I think about something my friend asked me. How many children I picture around myself at the hotel pool of my future. My friend's wife is pregnant with their third child. He wants to spawn as many children as he possibly can. Easy for a man to say. His body doesn't go through the process.

I don't have an answer to this. Instead of how many children I want, I'm thinking about how many Russians I want. Two or three would be nice.

Unfortunately, the only Russians I've met, the ones staying in the neighbouring hotel room, don't seem to understand my jokes about vodka. About Putin versus poutine, a Canadian delicacy of French fries, gravy, and cheese curd. Or why I have a men's sports jacket on. Quite the opposite of understanding, some sort of argument broke out. Hotel security arrived to escort the Russians out of the room. The room that belongs to them. I came here in the first place to ask for Pringles. My own room's snack fridge is empty because I ate everything.

Left inside their hotel room, with plenty of Pringles and chocolate milk, I wonder what Robert's up to.

Robert is the only person I told about this trip. In that version, I said something about a girlfriend named Jennifer. In reality this trip is sponsored by Jennifer's husband's friends.

I don't want to feel guilty about anything. Women know the type of men they marry. They know whether they are the type to sneak off to Miami with someone like me. This man tells all the Babies that I am his little sister. Women feel more comfortable with a guy who hangs out with a female relative. Because if you're hanging out with your little sister, it means you're not a total pig.

Evidently, everyone wants to feel more alluring. More than we actually are. Be it inside a nightclub, around a hotel pool, or at a celebrity chef's restaurant. Wanting to feel better is my day-to-day life. So I'm a natural at helping others do it for themselves.

With a purse full of glitter, I cast fantasy in Miami.

August 5, 2007

In the shadows, I meet a petite Venezuelan man. From his face, I see a life interrupted by hard partying. A collective result of late nights and exposure to the sun. He asks if I want to go somewhere private. I hop into his low-key hybrid 4-wheeler. We stop by the Mansion mega club to use the washroom. The immense line parts automatically for someone like this.

Away from South Beach we drive towards a collection of high rise condominiums. Here we transfer to a golf cart. We are at a marina. The interior of his home is minimalist and modern. Slick concrete is adorned with large pieces of art. And everything is white. Including the cocaine I spot like an outline of some unfinished sentence along the slate countertop.

There is an automatic cocaine dispensing machine. Like how someone might have a toaster.

My heart stops beating. A test of willpower. I excuse myself to the washroom. To breathe. A moment to remember. I do not need cocaine. It does not serve me.

Perhaps hash is permissible though.

We toke on oil and the pain in this man's face begins to intensify. Maybe he's killed before. Maybe he is dying. It haunts me to be smoking so casually with the Devil. Rather abruptly, I announce that I must go. Without bothering to take the golf cart to the gate, I begin to run. As fast and as far as I can.

19

HHH HHH HHH HHH IIII

"Existence without trust is walking knowingly into fires."

August 8, 2007

Back home, a local realtor propositions me to leave my mice and come work as his Buyer's Agent. He has a condo I can move into and a growing book of business. The money, he says, will speak for itself.

Since I need money, I'm saying yes.

September 6, 2007

Our real estate family is eccentric. On Saturday nights we attend Church and hold hands in prayer. Sometimes we finish the workday with a group hug. These events make me want to cry. These are colleagues but they feel like friends. Having new friends is overwhelming.

This realtor, my new boss, is someone to be close to. Our team reminds me that there are people in this world. It's because of this that I turn a blind eye to other things that go on. How we pretend to have offers on other agents' properties just to trick them. How we lie to people who ask us questions we don't know the answers to. How I'm instructed to find out who his girlfriend is having lunch with.

The first thing I've learned about real estate sales is that the best agents are the most charismatic. Integrity and trust go very far. So do adept liars.

September 24, 2007

If you desire money, it will arrive. In stacks of crisp bills. One thousand five hundred dollars dense. This money wasn't earned selling titled property, but by selling my body.

Even though I decided against outright prostitution, I've allowed Selene to broker the two of us on Craigslist to attract someone who wants to pay and see the live version of her and me together.

Agreeing to be a commodity, I wear an outfit similar to the images she put online. Lingerie, patent leather stilettos, thigh-high stockings.

I accompany Selene on a date in a man's living room. She and I sip wine until his art-deco glass coffee table becomes a stage. My dress drops to the floor and so do my inhibitions.

Show time has begun. The spectator, DP, online alias Doc Pleasure, is a Podiatrist slash Sex Freak who is paying Selene and me to fool around for him.

September 30, 2007

The period of rapid change is ongoing. The move into the high-rise apartment co-owned by my real estate boss is complete. With ample security to get in, I feel genuinely safe.

Work has been lucrative. Not just with Selene but also selling houses.

In the office, there's a wine cabinet. Out back, a hot tub. Aside from praying, there's hard work, fine dining, and also the occasional sleepover. We don't always pull wool over people eyes, but nothing is what it seems. By day, In Agency, people are one way. By night, or Outside Agency, an entirely different scenario exists.

It's all an illusion. We do what we do for money. For the bills I happen to be tucking inside a designer purse. It's Gucci, baby. And I love it.

October 1, 2007

Not everyone is interested in the kind of sex that people know as intercourse. For example, what Selene and I do with DP is different. We act out darker fantasies. It is fetishist, playful, vocal, dominating.

DP likes to be suffocated and slapped and fondled and teased and just slightly berated. Selene simply likes to orgasm. To do all this is something I am enjoying at the moment. And, as it turns out, DP pays generously.

October 20, 2007

Sometimes we deal with dishonest people and assume to be safe from their dishonesty. People tend to be consistent. If your colleague can lie to clients, he is just as able to lie to you. As a liar myself, I am hanging out with the right crowd.

Existence without trust is walking knowingly into fires. For whose entertainment this is, I don't know. The business of building a Real Estate business is similar to that of a Fire Department. Clients and prospective clients are arsonists. At any given moment, I drive around and put out the flames. I love it and I hate it and I do it all for free. Because in this game you never know which actions lead to getting paid.

This is called commission-based earnings.

Thankfully, the commissions are tallying up. When my boss asks if I want an advance payment on what I've earned, I tell him no. Hinting, he responds that he knows why I don't need a loan. That he knows how I finance myself. Hearing this, I falter under the notion that people will judge me. Trained as an illusionist now, I admit nothing.

There is nothing to admit.

October 21, 2007

We all have dirty secrets. Things are only as dirty as we deem them. In a world where people do some really awful things, to the environment, in sweat shops, and to animals, I've decided that what I choose to do with DP and Selene doesn't harm anyone. We are consensual adults. And my role in this is somehow therapeutic for me.

DP's penis doesn't go inside my body. This detail allows me to feel that I am not being paid for sex. I am being paid to act sometimes torturous, other times dramatically sensuous roles that I like acting in. For the moment.

Through my dates with DP, I begin to feel my fear of men slowly vanish. Something inside me that needed exercise, is getting it. Something inside of me that needed to exist, is.

I wish other people could easily understand this. Alternative therapy. I wish I could talk about it. Instead, I keep things private. More items in the vault. Ultimately, this means that Selene must be removed from the equation.

There has always been tension between us. And when people like us have a secret, one that others in general are not able to understand, the secret becomes powerful. And power corrupts.

Tension growing, Selene can sense that I want distance. She responds with threats to reveal me. Our friendship was never sustainable. Ending things with her will not be easy. But it needs to happen.

*

October 25, 2007
My boss' girlfriend, Barby, is a bit younger than Selene and me. She's either more naïve or better at acting innocent. I've been covertly stalking her. Then we all attempt to go out for drinks.

A recipe for disaster.

To avoid alcohol-induced confessions or drunken stupor, I go

115

home. Sometime after my departure, Barby runs over Selene in her car.

Selene is in the hospital. In the psychiatric ward. I receive a call explaining that the office has been vandalized. Barby is breaking up with my real estate boss. Or he is with her. And I am forbidden to continue as his associate if I wish to be friends with either of the girls.

For once the drama does not directly involve me, but I can't be happy about it. The decision of how to wash my hands, stay employed, and keep my friends must be made quickly. This is called an ultimatum.

There is a saying, something about not pooping in your own kitchen. My kitchen happens to belong to someone else. His is the hand that feeds me. And I have to clean up this shit.

First, I delete Selene. Our relationship was ending anyway. I do this through text and say she's become vile. Better than boring. A line from a movie. In reality, Selene isn't either of these things. She's just a liability. That I'm not insured for.

With or without coverage, a human can only handle so many liabilities. What to do about Barby, I will figure out later. After I eat an entire box of cookies.

October 31, 2007

Unhappy with the break-up, Selene threatens to expose my fandangle with DP. To my clients and to the entire city. Since she can't expose me without exposing herself, I try not to care.

On the road from rags to riches, absolutely everyone is willing to throw someone under a bus. To survive, one must become the driver or stay off the street.

*

November 11, 2007

On another vacation from my problems, I'm in Playa del Carmen, Mexico, with Travis. Even on a beach gazing out over turquoise ocean, drinking the best wine available, I need more. My anguish is real. Even here. In the safety of Travis's company. The illusion seems to be fading.

I ask him to go to the pharmacy and buy the strongest thing they sell. He returns with packages of Diazepam. Brand name, Valium.

I can't remember what this drug is for. I've heard of it. Not on the streets but back when I used to read psychology text books. Because of this I trust the medication. Not that I can deliberate about trust. On Valium, one or two pills later, I am fast asleep.

November 14, 2007

I suspect I am not fooling anyone. My real estate family have turned on me. I know it. Our clients are talking about me. Other realtors are talking about me. Everyone is talking about me. About how unprofessional and incapable I am.

November 26, 2007

I decide that I need a roommate more than I need business. Whether this is the right decision, who knows. That's the thing about burning bridges. Once they're gone, they're gone.

All I can do is look forward and assess whichever side I happen to be standing on. On this bank, the scenery is of another condo. Not a listing but one I'm moving into with my ex-real estate boss's now ex-girlfriend.

Having a friend down the hall is an opportunity to be honest. Being accountable to a real friend will force me to rebuild myself. To question some of my behaviours. To put me in a position where I can be influenced to be healthy.

Maybe I can transition from periodically hating myself to mostly respecting myself.

I'm probably expecting way too much out of my new friend. She also happens to work in property. She's good at her job. She only knows the side of me that I project, as an emerging and successful professional in the same field. She does not know about my entire recent past, or the Valium as self-medication *du jour*. Nor the fact that I have appointed her my newest saviour.

December 26, 2007

I did not spend Christmas with anyone because I'm stuck in another black hole. A blackness that devours everything. Even my parents' gift, a parcel of my favourite types of things, cannot distract from the nothingness of nebulousness. The safest and most dangerous place to be.

I find Valium to be helpful. After the stash from Mexico suddenly ran out, I had DP call in a prescription to the pharmacy across the street. Because he is a doctor, he can do this. Prescribe pain-killing medication.

Sedated, I cannot feel anything and sleep more. Waking up is heavy. Like stone. Somehow I'm even more tired than before.

December 27, 2007

I decide to text Mr. Evil Twin. He responds. I hint that I want him. Or that I think I do. I really have no idea because I am conflicted by his financial status. He is apparently a billionaire. A fact I learned from Travis.

Drawing a figure with a bunch of zeros on a piece of paper, he tried to explain the difference between a millionaire and a billionaire. I stared at the diagram, listening though unable to comprehend the intangible.

Through real estate sales, I'm learning about money. A knowledge that extends from three zeros to five. Thousands I get. Hundreds of thousands I get. Millions and billions are beyond me. But exceedingly attractive.

Money can buy you so much. The beautiful homes. The exotic African safari vacation. The lux furniture. Artwork. Dinner parties. The ten-car glass-enclosed garage. The in-house gym. Personal training. Heated toilet seats. An expansive garden. Spa treatments. I decide that I might like to buy these things.

Evil Twin's home is a lavish escape. The pumpkin-orange condo I'm leaving no longer feels new. It feels like something I should be disgusted with. Cheap laminate flooring and Ikea furnishings pale in comparison to hardwood and artisan Italian-made.

Because I like his environment, I settle for conversation and company with Mr. Evil Twin. I try to act contented and amused. An easy feat, up until he starts to talk about his newest charity. Raising money for battered women, cancer survivors, and sick children. Sitting in his kitchen, I sip tea and listen to him go on.

Instead of feeling congratulatory or proud, I remain sceptical. Brenna, who is working these days in a cancer research lab, voices many frustrations about research. About how their funding comes and goes. About how the work focuses less on a cure and is driven more by the publicity of where the research money came from. The marketing opportunity.

I sense a businessman who has found another profitable business model. I've nothing against capitalists. But, due to my past, the topic of battered women makes me uneasy.

Rapidly, I can't drink tea and stomach this man or his kitchen or this conversation. I need alcohol. And I need it now. He has nothing with an alcoholic content to offer me though. All of these assets but not a simple glass of wine in sight. I stare at a magazine on the countertop. The cover boasts a portrait of his face. Testament to his rising star. He opens the cupboard above and produces a bottle of white wine.

It's half empty.

Pouring me a glass of stale sauvignon blanc, he explains that it was left over from a dinner party. That he doesn't have more because he doesn't drink.

At all.

Suddenly, my jealously and frustration pause. It isn't his success or his hobbies bothering me. It's the mere fact, and a major reason for his ascent, that he isn't an alcoholic. For the first time ever, I wonder what life could be like sober and high-achieving. Excellence, it seems. Like Aristotle says, it is the behaviour we repeatedly practise.

What's possible to accomplish in a world without blackout drunken evenings or hangovers? Why is alcohol necessary for me to be close to someone? To actually keep me distant? What's the opposite of excellent? Questions swirling.

Answers can be a painful conundrum. I am not yet ready to face the evidence of sober success. So I fixate on how white wine should be kept. Namely in the fridge, not a cupboard. Desperate, I drink the warm wine on offer while pondering the photos of his children held with magnets to the fridge. The eldest looks roughly my age. I wonder why none of his children are here for the holidays.

He drops me home imparting a cellophane-wrapped gift basket. One of many someone like him receives over the holidays. I say thank you.

Once inside I eat a strange array of condiments and snacks from within the hamper, then throw up immediately afterwards.

I decide I want nothing to do with anyone linked to any sort of charity.

18

|||| |||| |||| |||| ||||

"A morning drunk is an easy target."

December 31, 2007

I had an immediate loyalty to Barby. I can't explain why. I just did.

We moved in, exchanged clothes, and went out. Neither of us took the time to brush our teeth. We laugh at this. Right into plastic cups of beer. We don't particularly like beer. And we also don't particularly like hockey. Though it seems we're at an exhibition hockey game.

It seems we're in similar shoes. Unsatisfied and wanting more. Tonight poses an opportunity to find something new. Something to change the sentiment of dissatisfaction into anything else.

Her current boyfriend, yet another real estate agent, is texting her.

Texts about kissing and getting together later. Barby turns to me. She looks sick. Not from the last swig of beer but because the texts are coming from five rows in front of us.

Her boyfriend is sitting there. Watching the game. To his right is another woman. One he is holding hands with. Her boyfriend is here on a date with his other girlfriend.

January 12, 2008

Living with Barby has resulted in a frenzy of nachos.

Sometimes we hate one another. Other times we laugh. We live a life of conspiring, lamenting, planning, crying, trying to sell real estate, and partying. Right now my clothes do not fit. Hers don't either. Owing, collectively, to about fourteen pounds of weight gain.

My top button open, I'm sitting on the couch. Barby looks at me. To share the news that she's pregnant.

I look at my plate of nachos. Hormonal influx explains a lot. I want to laugh at the absurdity of the situation. At the sympathy weight I've been gaining.

But it's her uterus that's occupied. Not mine. By something that partially belongs to the guy she's no longer seeing. Following the bust up on New Year's Eve, he continued a relationship with the other woman. A most unattractive and boring thing. Mousy blonde. Plain. Someone exactly opposite of Barby.

In her pain, I see frustration but also that her life will change. This could be a rock bottom. A humiliating place that will shock her onto a different path. The road someone takes at an accelerated pace, on the rise from a personal low.

She decides to turn to work. One of the top-selling agents in our brokerage wants to take her into his team. The deal board mounted in her bedroom has big numbers tallying up. She will motivate herself and do the work. And she will reap the benefits.

Though I left my role as buyer's agent, I still hold a license. But I am without a successful senior teammate to work alongside. Without these types of leads, I am at it alone. And struggling. In this regard, of smart career moves, Barby has become a big inspiration. Proof that hard work and focus can help outweigh suffering.

Before this can happen, we're heading to the bar to get extremely drunk.

She happens to be wearing an empire-waist, tunic-style shirt. Some realities can be hidden beneath baggy clothing.

January 15, 2008

I do not have a deal board with numbers on it. Breaking up from my previous professional affiliation appears to have been a premature decision. Because all of our business did not belong, in fact, to me.

I don't have the patience to rebuild any bridges. Mending a working relationship doesn't cross my mind. Mostly because the pain of being a zero is masked by Diazepam, and we're only as successful as the heart is happy. Mine's still broken.

Broke. Yes. Staying home. No.

January 19, 2008

I head west to Banff with another girlfriend, Mabel, to attend the Waterkeeper Alliance's fundraiser as her guest. My mission is an encounter with someone I met at the bar the other night. He introduced himself as Chief. A name that, upon hearing, made me want to know more. His real name turned out to be Chris. How underwhelming. Regardless, the feelings I get when I fall for someone new – they're still the best feelings I know. I want hold onto this feeling of love at first sight.

I arrive at the resort and Mr. Chris isn't returning my calls or my texts and I don't have a plan B so I explore the gala. In the washroom, Mabel throws talcum powder around the sink and mirror in a bizarre attempt to mask the snowstorm of cocaine that follows her. It dusts her face, her purse, her car, and the side table back in the hotel room. There's more of a blizzard by her than there is in all the Rocky Mountains.

Later I return to the hotel room to order a ham croissant from room service. Her stash of cocaine stares at me. I decide to indulge.

February 12, 2008

Before he became my role model, Chris became my world. He's beautiful. Loves his job. Loves his friends. Parties hard and has fun.

He is everything I want to be.

He also happens to be in a long-term relationship with someone else. This other woman he happens to live with. Because of this, our relationship is largely based on text message and email. A forum that allows us to proceed with caution. In electronic communication there is no tone and little context. In SMS, the ability to know what is actually going on is lost.

Without tactile communication, kinaesthetic people easily feel uncertain. Apparently I am kinaesthetic.

Lacking certainty, I continue to see DP on the side. Making money that way, I'm only so motivated to try and move real estate.

February 28, 2010

The fact that Chris has this other woman isn't ideal. It's likely her and I wouldn't get along as friends. In terms of fidelity, though, Chris and I equal, right? Because I have DP. And we, too, are uncommitted.

*

March 15, 2008

This current low is sub terrestrial. I want to give up. This decision came after drinking a 26er of vodka before 10 am. In a state of hopeless and pathetic drunken despair, Barby did not deliver a pep talk. Rather, she kicked me right in the shins.

A morning drunk is an easy target. I don't blame her.

I am a disappointment. My reputation is ruining her career and she can't be friends with me anymore. The main cause of her upset? I was late and then absent for several professional commitments.

Have I been making more serious bad decisions? I don't want to analyse my cause of failure. Surely as a solution someone else can take over my listings and active clients. Someone else can show up on time and prepared for work. Not me. Because I am finished. With this life. With everything.

In a parting effort, I email Chris. Immediately, he responds. Asking why I'm drinking alone in the morning. He counters that Barby is just upset with me. He tells me to make some phone calls and convey some plausible excuses to those I let down. To not let a few bad days ruin everything. He explains that if I do not buck up today, I might have regrets tomorrow.

In the email he tells me how he wishes he was here to hug me. That he misses me. That I should not give up. The exact words of encouragement that I need to hear. And that, on reading them, save me.

This is a form of honest love. Responding to an SOS.

Chris's intimate relationship with his Blackberry gets me through today. Instant messaging, a downfall in some aspects of communication, is also a means to rapid, honest, and eloquently written words. An ode to the futuristic poets and motivational speakers of the digital era. Not as good as a real hug. But effective, none the less.

I hurt too much to say how I really feel. A real and painful and devastating hurt is emerging. Whatever I've been numbing with recent pills is manifesting. It's leaking. Chris's questions are forcing me to contemplate what I'm doing wrong. Forcing me to feel. The moonlighting with DP. Enabling my girlfriend to use cocaine. Self-medicating with pills and alcohol. It all hurts.

I savour his email. The Band-Aid. In the shower I envision his hug. Then, put on make-up. And attire. And pull myself together to meet a new client. I take on two new listings. Side by side homes in a coveted inner-city neighbourhood. From this moment, Chris becomes my rock.

March 30, 2008

I know deep inside that Barby doesn't hate me. Despite what happened the other day. I wish I could tell her more. Instead she sees the surface. The partying. The breakdowns. The designer shoes. Our offices are side by side – she knows I haven't sold any homes lately. That I'm a zero. And broke. So she must wonder what the secret source of money is.

If being honest wouldn't risk abstractions of the truth getting out further, I'd gladly talk to her and tell her. About how I finance buying new things. But the vault is still locked. I repair the leak. And keep my secrets. Tightly concealed.

*

May 1, 2008

Everything around me is unravelling rather quickly. Mabel's SLX is smashed and she is in the hospital. For real. She had a seizure.

Using a lot of cocaine can do that.

In a phone call to her sister I explain that she needs help. To myself, I admit enabling her. We attempt an intervention. In the future, maybe it will be helpful. In the present moment, she is furious. I get home to an email from Mabel about several things that I am up to. She sent it to my parents and to Denton. It contains information about my relationships. Namely, about my new crush Chris plus my dealings with older men like the philanthropist, and DP.

Denton finds this information especially amusing and wastes no time forwarding it to the senior executive team at the philanthropist's financial stock brokerage and, of course, to Chris.

A spiralling momentum picks up as my private life becomes exposed. I can't tell the direction things are turning in.

May 10, 2008

In light of my girlfriend's overdose and the email scandal, Chris and I are done. But we're not done. I try to clean up the pieces of glass that are my charade without getting cut. A delicate act. One that takes all my energy and requires colourful distortions of the truth. Even I don't know what is and what isn't true anymore. I try but fail to fathom who is to blame for what, who is not to blame, why people need to blame others at all.

May 12, 2008

With a little liquid courage, I tell Chris that I have fallen in love with him. I've fallen and want to see where I land. That no matter where it is, I'm sure he'll be there too. Asking me what I'd like to drink.

Any love that requires a fall, that requires a drink, is not real love. It is dependency.

I have become just as dependent on Chris as I have been on other things. And he is dependent on me as well. So we work.

Two co-dependents.

17

‖‖ ‖‖ ‖‖ ‖‖ ‖‖‖

*"Everything about holding onto a past
is torturous and alienating."*

June 1, 2008

I moved from the apartment with Barby to the Deep South of Calgary on my own. It's rural. And quiet.

Jogging through surrounding farmland, I embrace solitude.

I accept that life is a hustle. With clients, with Chris. Looking around me gives a clear picture of what the world expects. Two-and-a-half stories. A two-car garage, one fast car and one utility. Three bedrooms and a bonus room. Children. A dog, optional. This is what the world expects. This is what people are supposed to aim for. I become familiar with all of these features. These homes. These couples. And I work with it. I do a series of deals. Nowhere around here do I see myself. The present or any future version. Despite that, I tell people like DP that I am done with the city, being terrified, provocative lingerie, drugs, and the past.

June 7, 2008

People here shop at outlet malls. The kind I hate. Walking through their massive aisles, I scan the shelves to envision how to decorate my next house. The one I've decided to save money to buy.

One of the aisles has a display of Yoga mats. I heard recently that Yoga can save the body from pain and anguish. I was encouraged to start a practice. Interesting advice. I refrain from announcing my long-learned tolerance for shin splints and decide to attend a class to see what it's like.

Hot Yoga reminds me of how I used to do lines of coke and then sit in an infra-red sauna. It is shockingly similar. Intense, sweaty, challenging. Perhaps a natural high. Precisely what I've been waiting for.

In class, my first discovery is how tight my hips are. Then, I faint. In some position called Camel. We started on our knees, then arched the back deeply. Everything went fuzzy. Then black. Maybe I pushed too far. Maybe I have too much pent-up emotion. It is too hot to know the cause.

Sweating profusely, I regain consciousness. It seems dropping my head back is too intense to handle. Tight hips and fainting. Yet more challenge in an already challenging life.

The instructor speaks of setting goals within the practice. Naturally, I vow to stop blacking out and to be able to remain in the boiling room for the duration of the class. Overheating is, apparently, mental. Just like instances in life, Hot Yoga can seem unbearable. Instead of quitting, we should lie down and relax through breathing. I'm not sure how people do this – relax in burning hell – but to pick up the trick could become a valuable tool.

*

July 13, 2008

Chris caught me leaving DP's house. Oops. The playtime money was hidden but the bogus Valium prescription wasn't.

Since I've changed my story so many times, I stick with the only one I know. The apology. I can apologise. So I do.

I tell Chris that I am sorry for lying, for seeking pharmaceuticals illegally, for communicating with another man. I apologise for my seeming apathy. I tell him that I might be sick. That I might not be sick. That right now I do not know who I am or what I am capable of. I tell him that I often live in a dark hole. That this place, and being sad, feels familiar. That I can't handle feeling any worse. That being on the diverted side of a broken relationship to him, delusional and helpless, will kill me.

I tell Chris that he keeps me going. That he gives me strength. That I survive on him. I tell him that I want to be better. That there is hope. That food has taste and a spectrum of colour exists. I beg him to see me again.

In my apology there are no lies.

I need Chris to survive right now. He must sense this. Because he agrees.

We get back together.

July 14, 2008

I continue to need Chris. But instead of coming to see me, he's out with friends. My mind plays back to his words telling me that we're over. The imagined rejection becomes real.

I ask if his friends are doing cocaine. He admits that yes, they are partying tonight. I swallow this and realise that him and I are two wrongs. Which, people say, don't make a right.

Even though I suspect that we are not right for one another, I cannot end things with him.

Instead, I wrap both my arms tightly around him and I hold on. He holds on back. Both of us desperately want the other to be holding on equally or even more tightly. Both of us loosen our grip in fear that this isn't true.

Letting go of someone is a nightmarish feeling. A dependent love weakened not by the knowledge but by the fear that the other is releasing their grip. The Chris I love is not the Chris I hold onto. Weakly. My happiness is not contingent on who he actually is, but on an illusion of who I want him to be. On the saviour I've made him out to be.

I will continue to violate Chris's expectations and, in turn, he will continue to violate mine.

In this battle, my heart falls clear out of my body and into his hands.

As a shell, I have three things. Hot Yoga. Real estate in the suburbs. Apologies.

For the things I've done that are wrong, I apologise.

July 15, 2008

Chris's rational mind is telling him to walk away from me. He knows that he will be disappointed by me time after time. But his heart, what drives him, will not let go. He begs me for reassurance. So, like any lover would, I give him my word. That I will stop. That I will change. That I will become idyllic. But these words are not mine. They're his.

*

July 26, 2008

Selling family housing in the suburbs is good to me. A sure ticket to make money with which to save most, spend some. On salon treatments, bottles of wine, shiny accessories, dresses, and party decorations. For future parties. I still just want to party. All the time.

My clients think that I live in one of these big houses. Which I do. What they don't know is that all of my things are in the garage. Waiting for the game of house to become real. Currently, I borrow an address from a client and live here for free. At 2,800 square feet this property is big enough for a family of seven, but this is the façade of success. An enormous house. A car that gets detailed on a bi-weekly basis. Shoes that cost more than six hundred dollars. Perfect lipstick. In reality, this house is leveraged on mortgage fraud. No one in their right mind would buy it at such an inflated price. I know this and use it to my advantage. And DP financed the shoes.

My sign out front serves as advertising. I walk past my things in the garage every day. All the things I bought to make me feel good about myself. Stacked in boxes. Meanwhile, I'm perfectly content with the sea of surrounding farmland and an air mattress set up off the kitchen. I prefer bare feet. I prefer no make-up at all.

July 31, 2008

I left giant house number one for the same thing in the next neighbourhood, built around a fake-lake pop-up community, to the east. This move is supposed to be a temporary arrangement. To live with my boyfriend. Chris. Who has finally left his other girlfriend.

We seem to be hanging out a lot. Going to the gym. Drinking. Clubbing. Going to dinner. Golfing. Taking trips at every opportunity. People call this a fast life and it's adorable. The ongoing honeymoon.

This honeymoon, however, does not signify the start of a marriage. There is no commitment. When I stop moving I notice my self-worth hanging. Mostly in the closet. But no one challenges being well dressed.

August 2, 2008

Something is indicated by all of the passwords. The locked email. The locked cell phones.

There are secrets.

We pretend to have a foundation built on something other

than mistrust. This is called denial. Its consistency is quick sand. A wet and dangerous thing that I've sunken into. Deep. Too deep to move.

Since Chris looks exactly like the type of guy I'm expected to be with, as long as I do what is expected, everything is fine.

The pretence of what a relationship, and a career, and a social life should be, seems simple. No one talks about Valium or the man who pays me to talk dirty to him. No one talks about the baggies of coke that I find in Chris's pocket. Or the other girl's phone numbers I find in the console of his Land Rover.

No one talks about these things.

August 13, 2008

Our honeymoon continues. On a whirlwind, we book a trip to Europe. I pick Istanbul. He picks Greece. We're going to meet his good friends from Australia. The clash of East and West. A distraction from something that has been growing inside me. For a while now.

Fatal jealously.

The vilest of poison. It has contaminated my being. It has become much larger than me. And it is festering. It's something so ugly that I can't bear to face it. So I wear my new Prada sunglasses, tailored dresses, and shimmery make-up. And I'm skinny, from all the Hot Yoga.

August 17, 2008

I never thought I'd be taking life advice from the lyrics of a Britney Spears song. The one about toxicity and slipping under.

Midnight rolls around. My boyfriend is out. Restlessly I walk the streets to where the new construction ends and the rolling hills begin. I can't help it. I call him and call him and call him.

Nothing in the air can distract me. There aren't any stars in the sky. Chris is not here. The sky is empty. The streets are silent. I'm here all alone.

Eventually he comes home. Floating up the stairs on a cloud. Twinkling. I lunge at this light. I don't know where it's been or who it's been with but his phone will tell me. So I lunge for his phone. His phone always knows. That he was calling someone else.

Beyond the fenced backyards and wide open spaces of the suburbs shrills the maniacal chase that follows my threats to kill someone.

He runs.

We both run.

We stop.

We're at a baseball field. Just sitting there. This part I remember. Sitting in the grass. What I don't remember is punching him in the face.

It dawns on me that the two of us just scheduled a European honeymoon. The title of the Facebook photo album I'll choose to omit would read something like:

This Is Not Normal Behaviour.

August 21, 2008

My mind stops racing enough to send Chris an email. To do what I know how. I send another apology.

I don't explain the comprehensive list of times I've been involved in violence. Forget Denton. And the high school girl fights. Those were organised as after school, or hockey game intermission, entertainment. Scraps really. And the time I clubbed a girl in the head with a giant sea kelp. Which was supposed to be funny.

Forgetting the gruesome is habitual for my recovery. Surely, minor violence, to a degree, is amusing. Wrestling matches.

Boxing. As a last resort, I try to make light of the situation with a joke. About how bad a punch I swing.

I repeat how much I admire him and his friends. And move on to how the womanizing slightly concerns me. Then I attempt to blame him for my actions.

That I have serious anger problems and have become insanely jealous, I neglect to mention. *Au contraire*, I reiterate how I want to inspire others to live a clean and healthy lifestyle. I tell him that him using drugs breaks my heart. Because I'm working so hard for my own sobriety.

I tell him all the things that I wish he was telling me.

Then I defend myself.

I tell him that he's not working out enough. That he's not helping me to get a house. And that by leaving other girl's phone numbers in the car, and in our bedroom, he is asking for trouble.

This is me trying to make him feel guilty. Even though I hit him. This is called manipulating.

I finish by telling him how lucky he is. That I could have hit harder. That poor aim and lack of force led to a crap punch. I then ask him what he wants to do.

His response is that he doesn't want to break up. Of course. By this point we're both fucked up.

August 23, 2008

The days go by and I keep apologising. I say that I'll never do it again. Which I really want to be true. Even though I know it's not.

August 28, 2008

When surrounded by corruption, you always look for more evidence. Something to make certain what you already know, that you should stop searching and walk away.

135

The investigations prevail. I don't trust Chris. And Chris doesn't trust me.

We both try, somewhat successfully, to hide the evidence of our problems by throwing a large blanket over the elephant in the room.

Though every once and a while his trunk reaches for a peanut.

Hiding any past that we haven't let go of is hard. Like spilling red wine. The liquid may dry but what is left behind is a telltale stain.

I'm covered in stains. And so is he.

Everything about holding onto a past is torturous and alienating. In search of a forum to be myself, uncensored, I've decided to seek the company of someone who knows my past. I call Selene. At her side, everything feels quite normal.

*

September 19, 2008

In Europe, Chris and I pretend that everything is fine. And in a lot of ways, on vacation, it is. We look good and people are nice to us. We party like reality TV stars. We drink expensive cocktails. I have no idea who is paying and it really doesn't matter. Bills don't arrive. As far as I'm concerned, the party won't stop. All over London. Istanbul. The Prince's Islands. Athens. Mykonos. It never stops.

Enclosed within the flat stone walls of a hammam bath house in old Istanbul, I see it in a reflection. In the women's quarters, separate from the men. Here on my own. Naked in a room of naked others, I can see that my being needs much more healing.

How to sit still in the vapour, evades me. How to breathe and relax, is impossible. How to wait for my turn to be washed in peace and tranquility, is foreign.

Scanning the other women in the room, I panic. I look for a clue about what I should be doing. The answer is so obvious. I should be doing nothing.

This is torturous.

My legs start to vibrate to imaginary dance music. I begin to pick at my mangled feet. They tell the tale of how hard I am on myself. I sit on a bench and repeatedly fill and empty the wash basin, desperately trying to wash away the restlessness. My heart winces. One of the bath moms approaches and tells me to stop.

My heart cries, embarrassed. Her words are truth.

To relax, I don't need to do anything. Stop. Please.

The emotion of having a Turkish woman wash and exfoliate me during the scrub down is tender. In the sponge and lather lies comfort. To be held in her arms is to remember what it's like to be a baby. Held in the arms of a loving soul.

This is called therapy of human contact.

Soul cleansing.

16

||||| ||||| ||||| ||||| |||||

*"For anyone who hates themselves,
a smack in the face is sobering."*

September 20, 2008

On returning from the trip I move in with Travis. To remain
undistracted while I look around and buy a place of my own.
A place of refuge. I tell everyone that the suburbs with Chris
became cramped. That I miss downtown. No one argues these
points.

The more I move, the less I see. It's like staring into the
distance from a moving car.

Travis agrees that a real estate investment is a good idea.
Something concrete. My Yoga teacher spoke about stability
in class. I begin to ponder commercial real estate instead of
residential. Maybe it's more stable. Either way I'm going to buy
something. And sell whatever else I can in the meantime.

October 10, 2008

It's not easy to create calm in chaos. Despite the sentiment that
I should try a new direction, old habits die hard and I continue
to go all over the place.

In Yoga postures like Tree pose, balancing on one leg with
arms stretched overhead, lives an idea that one can have a
balanced life. However, my tree teeters. It totters. It falls down.
But if I hold hands with the Yogi beside me, or focus on a point
ahead, the balance improves.

In the company of Selene, I look for clues on how to get my act together. Her new Mercedes Benz, new condo, bigger lips, blonde highlights, jewelry from Tiffany, and recent vacations to Malibu and Jamaica, seem to indicate the right path, but she doesn't seem entirely happy. Indeterminate energy. It's fragile.

Being with Selene is fun. She's funny. She's quite herself and has several great qualities. But it's also intense. And probably a bad idea.

October 11, 2008

Driving aimlessly, I decide to go to visit Denton. A stark contrast to the rampant dog-napping of past years. He's who dog sat for me while I went on holiday.

I just need to talk. This life is draining. I'm tired. Tired from all the driving, the scandals, being an outcast, my life without Chris, my life with Chris. Even though Denton doesn't have advice he always has a hug. In his embrace I feel love. The treacherous, awful love that I had to get away from, but also a true force. A strong and certain hug is one we should accept. If it's from someone like Denton, though, take the hug then fly away. So I let him hug me. Just long enough to feel it. Then, before anything else can happen, I leave. How I wish I had better options.

October 12, 2008

In the pit of my stomach, I feel ashamed. I'm still driving around without purpose. I've been driving all night long. The sun is rising and I'm terrified. I'm scared of being the type of person who cannot be alone. I go past the condo that I finally bought, and I stop to think about it.

Buying a house won't give me a home. It won't fix anything. Nowhere in the mortgage agreement is a clause to ensure the emotional wellbeing of the borrower. A condo and a mortgage aren't going to teach me how to relax, provide security, solve my relationship issues, or give me a proper hug.

I feel endangered. Scared. So I decide to get back together with Chris and propose that we move somewhere far away.

*

October 22, 2008

I forgot about the black eye. Until, from the corner of it, I catch the stinging glance of concern from other people.

Travis is in Cabo San Lucas with a new date, to enjoy the Pacific winds, waves, and Mexican tequila. For company, I invited Selene to watch the horse cutting performance classic. Beautiful horses and glamorous cowboys are suitable entertainment.

The evening commenced with her delivering a lecture on how I can do better than Chris. An opinion contrary to what I want to hear. A bottle of white wine served alternative consult.

At the arena we didn't see the rhinestone cowboys like the ones I envisioned. Instead, an array of pudgy mothers and their offspring. We tried to feel content simply observing the horses.

Cutting is a timed event where a rider has to separate a calf from the rest of its herd. Entertaining. For about fifteen minutes.

The tickets had us sitting in the sponsor section, up front, beside the cameras and among a crowd who all seemed to know one another. It was stressful. No one talked to us or the mini dresses we felt suitable to wear. The attention we were getting made me uncomfortable, and the attention we were not getting was even worse. To relax, I ordered a cocktail. The liquid disappeared from the glass. Then, we did too.

In Exhibition Hall West next door, the Rocky Mountain Food and Wine Festival was underway. There was free wine to sample, and opportunity to sample the people sampling the free wine. Immediately someone enthralled by Brazilian Acai berry import hovered in front of me. Then a small crowd. Like herded animals, we moved collectively towards the premium scotch.

Then Selene dragged me to a terribly depressing lounge. A place where no one dances and the music is average at best. Standing around a perfectly rectangular room became immediately claustrophobic. It was too loud to think, too loud to attempt conversation, and too dark to see. I headed to the disabled washroom.

This whole Yoga idea that you can breathe through discomfort seemed a good concept to test.

In and out. The breath came rapidly. I was hyperventilating. It wasn't calming at all. Rather, I was enraged. Against my rapid shallow breathing, my phone was buzzing with incoming texts from Selene. She can't find me and thinks I'm a sell-out bitch and other, more colourful, adjectives. Fired up, a seed planted somewhere deep in my subconscious grew into quite a bush. Picking the intoxicating fruit off a branch, I devoured it. It's taste and effect were exacerbated by wine, vodka, and scotch. It was time to stop Selene. I'd had enough of her bullying.

I emerged from the washroom to approach her. In a condescending tone, I told her that she has no business sending rude texts. She needs to get a grip.

Nearby stood DP. Conniving, I looked to him then turned to her. He's homage to the burden of shame. Neither of us wants to be seen in public near him. I called her a whore. Her eyes widened and her Juvéderm-enhanced mouth responded, threatening me. This is precisely when my vodka poured itself over her head.

Dirtied and in full attention of several onlookers, she grabbed me. We exited the lounge in a tussle. Out back, in the parking lot, with no one else around, the tension broke. All of it.

It broke as her tennis-playing forearm rocked my temple. It crumbled as her fist connected to my face. Again. And again. I stood there, leaning in slightly to each blow, wondering if hitting me makes Selene feel better about herself. Whether she likes hitting me as much as I like getting hit.

After the brawl, I side stepped past what was broken and walked to get in the car and drive home.

Mirror, mirror on the wall.

From the safety of the guest bedroom at Travis's, I looked like Frankenstein. Photo evidence was sent to Barby and Travis for comment. One more hit and my cheek would've split open. My eye is fat and my face puffy and lumpy. Rapidly, the skin darkened to deep purple. Shades of cabernet and shiraz.

This fight should have happened the minute I met Selene in Denton's bed. Sometimes getting hit is a good thing. For anyone who hates themselves, a smack in the face is sobering. I have become aware, finally, that the physical and the mental can hold hands. A marriage of pain. My masochism.

*

October 23, 2008

Whatever the pain has turned into. An avalanche. A catastrophe. I cannot endure it any longer. I want out. To erase the carnage. I want a new sensation. Yoga. Not that Hot Yoga but something else. Something soft and gentle and loving.

This is therapy. This is real Yoga.

In a candle-lit room, beaten, I am myself. It's 5 am. Blocks and pillows support my body. A blanket keeps me warm. The movements are subtle but the stiffness is excruciating.

In a candle-lit room, I cry. A cascade of tears from deep inside my soul pours onto the floor. I shut my eyes tightly. It hurts. Not just my bruised face but my entire recent life. Eyes closed, I look inwards. The scenery is overwhelming. Adjusting my spine, I continue to observe. The vault releases.

In a candle-lit room, I leave the locks and keys behind. I unload the vault. It sits on cork flooring beside a Ganesh statue. There are no more secrets.

October 24, 2008

I decide not to close on the condo I bought. But I am going to move. Not across the world or even the country. But to a whole new city.

Chris agrees that I should pack up, leave everything behind, start afresh, and not look back. I used to think that to leave meant to be defeated. It does mean forfeiting the down payment, the bulk of my life's savings. But that seems a small price to pay in the grand scheme of things.

Maybe I had it all wrong. To stay here is to be defeated. To leave is to grow.

It is time to let go.

One. Finger. At. A. Time.

15

‖‖ ‖‖ ‖‖ ‖‖ ‖‖

*"The whole world watches the news,
blind to the real circumstance of humanity."*

October 27, 2008

I place all the stones I've been holding onto into just one canoe
and row westward. Staying afloat while transporting a pile of
rocks, two dogs, an on-again-off-again boyfriend, a collection of
homeware, and a huge wardrobe is nothing less than miraculous.

People hear words about how happy I am to adventure into
new territory. A place where adaptation and flexibility will be
forced. The things that come part and parcel with a new place.
To change we must see past the new surface and look at the
reflection it casts. Energy that bounces, transmits, and refracts.
It seems that I will either be content with what I discover or
keep moving.

Someone who lives a charade cannot simply pull the plug on
the act by moving to a new city. It's like the party got cancelled
and no one kept the rest of me informed.

Despite this, a really posh townhouse is available to rent for
more than I can afford. It's in proximity to several Yoga studios
and other trendy Downtown things. Only one person asks about
the black eye, so I say nothing and sign a lease.

Chris, who might be my knight in shining armour, voices
his intention to take up my proposal and follow me. Evidently
a magical kingdom promises a new relationship for us void of
trust issues.

October 29, 2008

I have not yet experienced *Shavasana*, the relaxation pose at the end of class. When given the option to stay back and relax longer, a minute seems a century. Concentrating on how to relax causes unparalleled stress so I roll up my mat and leave disruptively. Encouragingly, select teachers continue to tell me to focus on the now. It's a time and place that I am eager to know. Achieved with a mind not governed by the past or thinking about the future.

November 8, 2008

After forking over what remains in terms of my own money on a mattress, riding boots, damage deposit, and the first and last month's rent, this abode lacks nothing but a chandelier. There's nothing to swing from. But drips of illuminated crystals can wait. For now other beautiful things that suit a townhouse in False Creek have found a home. By moving here I shall sever all ties with the past.

On most days it's cloudy. That's how Vancouver is. The reduced natural light seeps in from the floor-to-ceiling windows, brightened by light pine floors and white walls. Mint green glass accents compliment the zen interior design. Even the cabinets are seamless. There are no cracks in which to hide.

A park-level view and proximity to the ocean tells me that this arrangement is perfect. And, also, sink or swim. Jobless, it's either a high-achieving mind or a traumatized one that demands the risk of unaffordable luxury. In my case, both.

November 21, 2008

According to the news, there is some sort of global recession affecting the economy. Just not in ways that I can see. The price of my rent didn't go down. My car lease is the same.

More and more, the news has become a fortress of negativity

disguised in ways to make people feel better about it. The whole world watches the news, blind to the real circumstance of humanity. Don't watch too much televised news. Watch people. The ones around you.

December 7, 2008

A grimace permanently held by thin lips sits across from me. It almost transitions as she welcomes me to the team as an advertising executive. Foregoing the telltale upward curvature of sincerity or a smile, these lips shrivel immediately into a bleak line of coral shade lipstick.

My new boss looks at me.

Working Monday to Friday is my best plan to afford rent. Moonlighting as a waitress serves as insurance. Chris's plan is to lease his own ridiculously expensive townhouse, five blocks away. So much for a strong relationship.

It's going to be a long winter.

*

January 24, 2009

I didn't anticipate being over the party scene. It just happened. Honestly, there was no time to figure out why. Working, Mondays to Fridays, then Fridays to Sundays, the weeks pass by.

February 24, 2009

I quit my weekend job, which I need to get by, to make time for swinging Prada off my forearm and the possibility for spontaneous vacations. Time has a surreal quality in that nothing seems to make it viable. Venturing to a six-star hotel in downtown Seattle for a long weekend, I try out contrast.

From the soaker tub, I sip pinot noir, press against the jets, and try to envision how to be happy. Chris returns to the room, cancelling the debate. Abruptly, I learn that Sashimi cut her paw on the hotel escalator. Chris is racing to animal emergency while I await logic. A reminder that there's no point in planning beyond the moment. Or the blood. My wine, of co-conspiring shade, loses appeal.

Everything about this weekend away has no appeal. I suspect my future weekends will revert to serving food and drinks to paying customers. Less chance for personal emergencies.

May 11, 2009

I have read about bi-polarity. I read about someone who learned to view his personality as an integral part of his disposition. The extremes became not two opposites, not manic and depressive as some schools of thought indicate, but one. Flavourful terms to describe a vast and complex bouquet.

I'm starting to recognise that emotions can be extreme and also part of a continuum. Like a full-sized race track versus a miniature version. The former covers more distance.

Like how some parts of the world experience the same kind of weather year-round and some do not. Personalities are this way too. Some are more tropical. In the tropics, there are occasional storms.

Perception, it turns out, it a tricky thing. The human condition, reinforced by our language, creates a method of understanding where all things must have an opposite. Up versus down, black versus white, old versus young, round versus square, loud versus quiet, red versus green. Me versus you. Everything must have its opposite in order to be understood.

Except there is no such thing as a real opposite. To anything.

By re-defining how we categorize things, we can change how we feel.

As time goes by, through Yoga I notice that my hips aren't in pain. My spine doesn't kill me. I'm certainly not flexible yet but my knees start to relax closer to the floor. My spine can arch or curve forward without intense discomfort. In Butterfly pose, where we sit with a diamond shape between our legs, feet pressed together, and let our knees relax towards the ground, I decide that it is absurd to define the mind as two of anything.

Everyone's mind, and capacity to think and feel emotions, is just a range. A range, which is one.

Two supposed opposites can exist within one another. This is a paradox. And also reality.

I bow my head forwards and slide my hands along my legs to my feet. Pulling, the stretch intensifies. The teacher approaches. She touches my gripped hands and invites me to stop pulling. The pose isn't an act of force. My breath and gravity and time are all I need. Where I'm at is perfect.

I let go.

Low days are not separate from high days but a part of them. Low and high can coexist as the same thing. My head begins to relax. My chin touches my chest and my upper body lowers a few millimetres. My mind begins to relax and arrives at a place without deviance and without shame.

Inhale.

I want to be happy.

Exhale.

The pursuit of happiness can be upstream. Just like many fish swim as a battle to spawn. My girlfriend Lana said she'd rather live on a rollercoaster than a merry-go-round. In terms of my own understanding, in this pursuit or upstream swim, whatever we want to call it, life can be a rollercoaster. Embrace it. Ride it. Keep breathing.

The highest point offers the best vantage. The lowest is

reached following an almighty rush. These contrasts are amazing.

Rhythmic.

Breathe in.

Breathe out.

May 15, 2009

Someone once said that people love you for who you pretend to be. To keep their love, you keep pretending and performing and eventually you fall in love with your own pretense. This locks us in an image and as an act. People get so used to their image, their act, that they grow attached to the mask and disguise, and forget who they really are.

I can't tell if I've forgotten who I was or grew out of who I used to be.

Crouched in a low squat, my legs are wide and my elbows press into my knees. I look forward and place my palms on the floor for support. It's possible to balance the knees onto the upper arms and lift into Crow pose. A wise bird. My knees slip.

The fall is short and the mat is soft. Instead of failure, I think about Chris. About how I'm going to stop trying to change him. In these movements, attempting to balance and fly, it becomes obvious that changing anyone or anything other than yourself is impossible. No one has the power to do that.

Eventually, I will be able to fly as a crow. Strong and balanced. But I cannot change the world. Cultivation and sharing are the only possibilities. This hobby, Yoga, continues to offer me an embrace. I will leave the studio, see Chris, and share a smile.

When our partner smiles, we smile. When our partner is stressed, so are we. Learning to share emotions is important. Hidden under the mask I've come to wear for him, it's impossible to share fully.

We transition onto our backs and spread our legs and arms out wide. Palms facing up. The sound of a sitar sings to my memories. How we met. I reminisce about all the things that attracted me to him. The partying. The affair. How they used to be so alluring. I consider how they've turned into that which I can no longer condone. How they are exactly the things that will be the end of us. To a harmony of distant chanting, I close my eyes.

Lying in Corpse pose in a final rest, during which no one wears a mask, my mind becomes still and my thoughts begin to settle. One thought floats to the surface. One of such blindingly obvious merit, it is almost comical that it has only now entered my consciousness. Moving six hundred miles is a hell of a long distance to transport all of my shit.

I roll up the mat and replace the mask. It shows a smile that matches the real one underneath.

14

IIII IIII IIII IIII IIII

"Since forgiveness is an inward act of love,
if you're out of practice on how to love yourself,
inward love feels like being skinned alive."

May 17, 2009

I still have a habit of acting impulsively, mostly regarding the purchase of new clothes. My mind likes to exist sometimes inside a shopping bag. Four walls of separation from Chris-gate. People do not question my want of everything that is reasonable to want, but the real reason behind my retail therapy has to be more. It's not actually helping anything.

Ending a relationship is not easy. It is sad, scary, and hard. Learning to love thy self requires totally letting go and simultaneously opening up. An endeavour of adaptation, fitness, timing, and willingness.

I'm out with friends. Seems I have a few of those. Thank goodness. We are inside a large barn at the Cloverdale Rodeo. I see plaid shirts, jean shorts, and a personal arena in which to practise the splits. I'm ready to have a talk with Chris so dial his number. He answers. Except it's a girl, not him. I hang up. My call is eventually returned by someone incapable of rational adult conversation. His words are foreign, chemical, and high. Chris is cheating on me right now. With the girl and with a mind-altering substance. Never before have I felt so far away from him.

May 23, 2009

A salt breeze on my shoulders and a citrus wine on my lips feel like relaxation. With my visiting parents glancing disapprovingly across the table, a martini disappears. My parents don't drink.

Later, music plays. The dancefloor is a trance, strobe lights fight like interplanetary weapons against dozens of moving bodies.

Since two to a men's washroom stall is against the rules, commotion ensues. We are both swiftly escorted out of the club and into the street in front. I don't remember exactly what happened next but the fighting stopped here. There's no point in resisting arrest. I've just been busted. And tossed onto tacky linoleum floor. Garish lighting illuminates a real humiliation. I've not managed to break up with Chris or discuss what it felt like when the mystery woman answered his phone the other night. I'm not getting those things done.

But I am visiting jail for the last time.

May 24, 2009

Released, there isn't time to stall. I hail a taxi home and immediately seek refuge in my make-up bag. Into mid-height heels I slide, then pass by a reflection in the mirror. Someone in all black. A standard waitress look. To the Pirate Pub she saunters. A place on the waterfront boasting a tranquil view and fun ambience. Whether I meet good people or make decent money in tips tonight doesn't matter. These are no longer my priorities. I'm just thankful to be making it into work.

Instead of work I can't help but picture myself heading to an intervention. A sombre image.

My parents, instead of discussing what happened last night, elected to leave town before my release. If they drive non-stop, in eighteen hours and fifty minutes, they can forget. Laissez-faire. Their noninterventionism.

The only person to offer console is actually Chris. The target of last night's projectile cell phone. Or so called Assault.

In an email, Chris tells me how awful he feels. Seeing me detained, hearing my cries, and being helpless about a release from jail traumatized him. Apparently, it was a wake-up call to take better care of me because he doesn't want to lose me again.

Chris's comforting and tender words don't suggest what tools I can employ to prevent future arrests. To help me help myself. He isn't the one who needs encouragement.

Being that there's no phone in a jail cell, and being that my phone broke during the altercation, I missed the metaphorical wake-up call. Looking at the ruptured pieces that surround me, there's broken and then there's really broken.

My relationship falls under both categories. The one with Chris, and my behaviour when I've had too much alcohol.

Under mineral make-up I can approach tables to casually serve brunch to the good people of Vancouver. To revoke denial, an item I have removed from the menu, I share my situation with select colleagues. Chewing on blunt honesty, we wash it down with black coffee. A surprisingly palatable combination.

For this mess, a broom won't suffice. Instead, a motor based on airplane engine technology is required. Thank you, Dyson. With this vacuum, the mess disappears. And my intention to get help does not.

May 29, 2009

I sit in the car, sipping coffee. It's twenty minutes before my next therapy session. Ironically, this is exactly what I need. Not caffeine, therapy. It's mandated by the court, which forces me to participate. It's becoming obvious that my friends and family remain silent about my indecent behaviour because they are my friends and family, not the law or registered therapists.

For certain matters, like facing an Assault charge, professional help should be sought.

In the first counselling session, I rehashed events without metaphor or prose. How on Saturday night I began with drinks at home, then at Chris's house. How on most evenings, I drink. How we went clubbing on Granville Street. How this is standard. How even though I suspect him of infidelity right now, Chris removed my cell phone from my purse and jaunted with it into the men's washroom. How I followed. How a bouncer tried to intervene but I stood my ground. How it's not acceptable for Chris to go through my personal things. How even more inappropriate was the tone our drunken discussion about fidelity had taken. How music blasted as we fought loudly over who was to blame.

How, frustrated, the phone flew. Then my fists.

Ma'am, we just saw you assault that man.

These words, uttered by the police, made me stop immediately. Not that there's much choice when your arms are behind your back and handcuffs are being clinched tightly, ripping your skin. Ergonomic incompatibility for bony wrists. It felt just like the last time I was handcuffed. Déjà vu.

My mouth wanted to scream because the upcoming round of hellish torture, the pending nightmare, is one I knew. As they loaded me into a paddy wagon, I calmly explained that I couldn't be in a room with other prisoners. I didn't mention my last trip to jail or the traumatic crack-slap. It turns out that systems exist to reveal some of that, anyway.

I wasn't thinking about the penile system while sitting in the loading bay. Depressed. I managed to share that I might try to kill myself. A nurse brought me pills and someone else brought a bright orange jumper. Restrained inside it, I was led into a cell. All alone. Four walls padded with blue gym mattresses.

Mentally, I could not handle what was happening. Even my hands were jailed inside the jumper. On my side, in a fetal position, I lay on the floor and stared at the wall. The blue faded.

*

June 7, 2009

Not that I deserve it, but Chris took me on a small weekend vacation. He's out golfing. In the sand bunker that separates the sixth and seventh holes, I watch preppy golfers navigate manicured grass and water features. An iron or a wood, their only decision. In the trap, I bury what's left of my personal conflict and return to the lakeside penthouse. By dressing up for tonight, in a floral mini dress, I pretend to have poise and confidence. What was faceless, crawling, and shattered got left among errant golf balls deep in the back nine.

I beg Chris to lie down with me.

He doesn't.

My video camera, on record, captures how alien drugs make things. Visual evidence is a salient reference. The weekend goes by and the party's ongoing. So is the camera. The birthday boy, smiling softly, looks at me. His mouth opens and he's telling me he loves me.

The camera points away, cutting him off. I don't feel it. I don't feel anything but breeze off the lake. There are certain things a camera can't catch. Emotions of turmoil slowly coming to an end.

*

June 19, 2009

From the center of her dark brown leather couch, my psychologist, in front of me, has compassion. It's terrifying and I

155

can't bear to look back at it. At her. Tears stream down my face. Not a waterfall but a steady trickle. Beyond the blurry wetness is a single piece of paper. I've scrawled three words. My hands tremble and I repeat.

I forgive myself.

If I can believe these three words then I can be whole again. I must forgive myself. The court and legal system are willing to forgive me. They view participation with therapy as an Alternative Resolution. A satisfactory consequence to throwing a cell phone at the likes of Chris. My colleagues and friends also seem willing to forgive. But even though others are willing to forgive me, I must show responsibility for my actions and make more effort to get help.

Forgiving myself, it turns out, is the hardest part. Simply saying the words aloud feels venomous.

Since forgiveness is an inward act of love, if you're out of practice on how to love yourself, inward love feels like being skinned alive. It's to be vulnerable. It's to rely on the unreliable. It's like being sent out into the elements, unprepared, and expecting abuse.

The psychologist touches my forearm. I want to let her but I can't. It recoils close to my body. I need to repeat these words indefinitely until I believe them. From her mouth they seem less and less volatile and, eventually, the stinging stops.

She explains that some decisions are simply as good as the realities we are presented with. From her perspective, not all of my realities have been stable. My actions, given the cards I've been dealt, were reasonable. That in time I can get better at playing my hands.

Then the game will change.

Her council sounds similar to my favourite Yoga teacher, and Kenny Rogers' *The Gambler*. I can learn how to hold them, fold them, walk away, and run. I can count my money under the table and move forward, with a new reality and new decision making skills. This is moderation.

When our instincts and self-awareness exist in a healthy place, we can react to things in a healthy way. And there's no way I can handle another brush with the law for erratic behaviour. No time for counting when the dealing is done.

I need to forgive myself.

13

‖‖ ‖‖ ‖‖ ‖‖ ‖‖ |

*"I cannot feel at peace
when it takes so much effort to feel stable."*

July 6, 2009

Tucked in my luggage, along with cowboy hats and boots, is a list of rules. I'm going to revisit Calgary and her rambunctious Stampede and also attend a wedding. I need this list in order to manage myself in a tricky environment. Guidelines on moderation.

The wedding is of two people I know from high school. Some of the guests will be impossible for me to hide from. I suspect people who knew me well years ago can see right through me now. No amount of sparkle on my dress can create opacity. And I'm wearing a very sparkly dress.

Stampeding poses every risk. To drink too much. To become violent or angry. To behave in self-harming ways.

My list helps to mitigate inherent risk. It dictates rules of consumption. A beverage regulator. Zero tolerance for drugs. No swearing. I am to walk away from conflict. Go home. Sleep it off. And take walks along the river.

Responsible for implementing the list of rules, is me. Our own legs support our own body. The right leg steps back wide into Warrior One. The front knee bends and the arms extend upwards. The palms pivot and the chest opens up to the sky. She becomes devotional. Praising a sandwich. One that I left the party to come and eat.

Eating settles me down. Chris no longer can. He's still my rock though, too heavy to throw away. I bite into the sandwich and decide to unanchor myself. Emotionally. I do this. And nothing happens. No mass tide sweeps me away. I'm not drowning. I haven't fallen sideways.

I'm just standing here, eating a sandwich, and taking a pause to practise Yoga postures.

The real warrior is emerging.

*

July 31, 2009

The reason why so many people lose it on the weekends has to do with the typical Monday-to-Friday, nine-to-five schedule. People put themselves on hold during the week. Their bodies show up to work. Like robots. Robots who need an outlet come 5 pm each and every Friday.

August 1, 2009

I cannot feel at peace when it takes so much effort to feel stable. Working so hard to scrape by is not living.

Thankfully, forgiveness came.

Feeling skinned alive eventually subsided. A subtle transformation started with the shedding of layers of my being into the universe. Similar to that of a snake. The shedding of old skin. I imagine the old, what I am growing out of, fertilising the earth and growing into a flower. A Yoga teacher once told me that the things that we unload may be toxic to hold onto. Released, they go to where they are needed and can produce something truly beautiful.

Underneath, the person emerging isn't scared of self-respect and self-love. Maybe these things aren't unreliable. Maybe, they're the opposite. Daily. Never-ending. A certainty.

Transformation can be a natural process. In my case, catalysts existed. To lend a helping hand, provide a soft tug, act as a mirror. Whether I started this metamorphosis or not, I vow to take responsibility. No longer does saying this feel like an admission of guilt. I am not guilty. This I maintain. But I am responsible.

Looking at myself in the studio mirror, I wholeheartedly commit to overcoming fear and emotion. By saying it aloud, it becomes a Mantra.

Say what you need to say. Out loud. Say it at first to yourself. Then be brave and share.

*

August 5, 2009

A heart attack acts as a reminder to maintain good humour despite life's ups and downs. Travis went down. The creakiest wheel gets the grease, his advice on how to get service in the hospital.

He told me he will escape as soon as possible. Though what no one can escape, even Travis, is how fragile the heart really is. Like a seedling, the heart needs sunlight, fresh water, and fertile soil to grow. It needs Love.

Environmental love, the sun, kisses me. Intimately it warms my own heart. On the shores of Sandy Cove beach, in West Vancouver, I have an epiphany. About how desirable the real estate around here is.

August 15, 2009

More clarity is arriving. Mocking me because, visually, my eyes gave out. This is called iritis. Stress has given me a pesky ulcer in my eye. With it, physical vision is painful and blurry.

In a haze, I was unable to establish that the lipstick I've been wearing looks like an atrocious frosting of Pepto-Bismol.

However, I was able to re-establish a real estate license. In both respects, make-up and employment, I am no longer nervous of change. Change is the necessary means to end my current identity crisis.

Changing your professional title, a word that can be used to describe yourself, isn't true change because it is something outward. But, it's a baby step.

Having a label that works is an important tool to use if you can find a fit. Because labels affect our actions. Our behaviour can start to match any title we give our self.

I'm not waiting for anyone to appoint me as the type of person I want to be.

If you want to be funny, tell the world you are a comedian and start making some jokes.

I am aware that Realtor is just a label, but it happens to be better than Advertising Executive or Bartender. Or Party Girl. Or Connoisseur of Avoiding Criminal Charges.

The inability to see, it turns out, is a blessing in disguise.

Slowly, my gaze is shifting inward.

August 25, 2009

I remain detached from Chris. What I used to think of as a rock has transformed into a feather. A few gusts of wind and he is sure to blow away. I'll let nature take care of how things shall fall.

More mistral than breeze, the 2010 Vancouver Winter Olympic and Paralympic Games are shifting the real estate market. Specifically, my rental home has been sold to new owners. Finding a new place given the influx of visitors will be impossible.

Storm shutters closed, I tuck the feather into my hat. Chris can't drift away yet because I need to live with him. My solution to impending homelessness.

September 4, 2009

On my final day at the advertising office, my boss did not deliver any words of encouragement. Instead, snide words wishing me inevitable failure. All the more confirmation that departing is the right move. Escaping her negativity.

My internal voice is small but reminds me to see the positive. Beyond this small voice is something bigger. The knowledge that success is an outcome based on something invisible. It comes from integrity.

To regrow a voice, homework helps. Things like karaoke or, in my case, chanting. To match our inward projections with the outward ones. Do homework on the topics you need to. I'm starting to feel proud. For listening to myself and tuning out the others.

This is a glimpse at authentic decision making.

Just as it is impossible to distinguish from looking at a handle what it's attached to, the overall picture is not yet apparent to me. My hand presses down on a long golden latch and opens a door. A light shines through the doorway. A light I will take on the road with me. Leading both towards life and away from it.

12

||||| ||||| ||||| ||||| ||||| |

"Before you can balance, you must focus."

September 10, 2009

Moving in with your ex-boyfriend is stressful. My eyesight, already impaired, suffers the consequence.

Pain is a tightrope. Walking along it with precaution and instinct, I proceed. Typically, no one teaches us the intricacies of tightrope walking. There are few schools for acrobats besides those made eminent by Cirque Du Soleil. As an amateur in a three-ringed circus, I lean on Yoga. In Warrior Three, standing on one leg with the other extended back like an airplane, wavering, I look down.

Before you can balance, you must focus. In pain, it's impossible to focus on anything else. Below me I see the rope. It seems there are only two options. To dazzle or to plummet. Spectators that rim this circus arena are just as interested in a performer's success as they are in the possibility of gruesome satisfaction. A fall. Failure.

January 20, 2010

In ode to Jay-Z, whose ninety-nine problems do not include a woman, I'd like to comment on what remain as mine. Nothing to do with women either. But sandwiches. As my go-to tactic for abandoning people whose parties take a turn to drug-use.

Most recently, a New Year's Eve concoction. I left Chris and our friends behind to recluse at the Empress Hotel in Victoria Harbour. I sat in the window sill, peering out at ivy. Vines too delicate to climb. A stately knock at the door, then coattails, saved me from pondering a leap.

Once again, rescued by a ham sandwich.

In life, at any given time, we may have ninety-nine problems. Effective tonight, I refuse to let anything served at a deli be one of them. I want this to be the end of my emotional eating. Unfortunately, I have no idea how many croissants exist in the future.

February 10, 2010

Even though many are hard-to-sell buildings – one with a dilapidated roof, another with hundreds of thousands of dollars' worth of flooding damage, and a third with a stinky tenant – my listings are selling and my phone is ringing. On a career high I have presentations, showings, and marketing initiatives, and I am preparing to sell an immaculate harbourside penthouse and two oceanfront homes.

Million-dollar luxury real estate clientele, an updated website, shiny business cards, a three-figure cell phone bill, and a growing wardrobe indicate success. A tiny feather, flapping rapidly in thin air, is weak.

February 12, 2010

After learning about the aforementioned waterfront properties, my boss recommended that I entertain an inside deal and sell to a colleague's client. Foregoing public marketing is one way to make fast money. The catch, my colleague wants more commission than the typical split.

Why should I forego what the contract provides? My boss

answers to say that there are snakes in the grass. In my head I tell myself that it takes one to know one and that I'm not scared of anybody these days. I want as much money as I can get. I want what I'm entitled to. Instead of arguing, I nod and remain outwardly quiet. My gut is telling me to ignore greed and proceed with this thing called integrity. Which is how I've been getting all this business in the first place.

Ruffling feathers isn't an option for someone lacking her own plumage. I'm also lacking in a car. My lease expired and I handed my previous one in. And didn't sort out the next commitment.

Later, over hot green tea at the Terminal City Club, my client and I discuss the inside offer, go over paperwork, and speculate.

The potential buyer is in Las Vegas. A location that seriously hinders effecting a valid real estate transaction of this magnitude.

I don't try to understand the urgency or ask questions. Instead, I carry on, have the paperwork signed, and leave.

Carless, I walk along West Georgia to the corner at Hornby. Shining like medallions of encouragement and even more fragrant, I select twelve yellow roses. Sometimes, when the going gets tough, the tough buy flowers.

Flowers attract bees which are rare because they're going extinct. Saving the apiculture discussions for later, I follow the man interested in my flowers into the Four Seasons lobby nearby. His name is Sam he's old enough to be on the return to childishness. Tall. Slim. And effortlessly chic. He's after some pinot gris. And I, the business centre's fax machine and the possibility of sound advice. Nothing honey-coated.

After several glasses of pale yellow truth serum, I begin to reveal the things that are weighing me down. Things that I have not been able to share with anybody. Namely, about how I am trying to avoid a personal meltdown and execute a million-dollar real estate transaction. A deal that could be a golden ticket. To having my own place to live. A new car. Etcetera. Sam listens without expression. As if he is totally unimpressed by the scope of my potential dealings. As a matter of fact, nothing impresses Sam. Indifference. A quality that, in this moment, I find quite impressive.

He does not question why I can't afford a cab. He does not press for details about why I am carless. He doesn't ask about my ex-boyfriend. Or why I live with an ex-boyfriend. He doesn't ask anything. Instead, he hands me the keys to his BMW X5. Apparently he barely uses it.

I decide to like Sam. His taste in wine, immaculate, is a plus. He knows when to roll the dice.

February 14, 2010

Being busy with work leads people to expect that I'm fine. I expect Valentine's Day to involve jewelry. Van Cleef & Arpels black onyx calibre. But I'm not fine and the only jewelry I'm wearing is a stream of tears. Lying in these saline jewels in Chris's bed, I drown.

Here things are really hard. Due to the Olympics, Chris is hosting a barrage of visitors. His friends are loud and obnoxious and never-ending. They want to party. They want to get high.

It seems like the real athletic feat at the Olympic Games is the million-litre filter, an event performed by elite livers city-wide. Absolutely everyone is out getting pissed drunk, all day long. I'm in the mood for none of it. I want to get ahead.

I'm not crying alone either because one of Chris's friends just attempted to embrace me. A hug or something else. I can't tell, but proximity to anyone at the moment is more than disgusting. I'm furious. Instead of assaulting him, I opt to go outside for fresh air. I stand on the terrace and immediately spot the large stash of cocaine, poorly hidden in the planter.

166

February 23, 2010

The tension at my estranged lover's townhouse is so thick you would need a butcher's knife to cut through it. A utensil I am glad doesn't exist in the kitchen, because I'm left to casually introduce myself as the ex-girlfriend and roommate to the other women he's started to bring home.

Thankfully I still have work to focus on and leave to look for a Mandarin translator. The good natured non-English-speaking client of mine deserves attention. The silence of a language barrier is perfect retribution to personal crisis. Operation putting-my-personal-life-on-pause until, at the very least, I have a new place to live, seems to be working.

Miss Real Estate's on fire.

*

February 28, 2010

I really, really do not trust myself to keep everything together. Surely life would be easier on medication. I long for some pain killers. Unfortunately, the only doctor I know is naturopathic. Desperate, I'm willing to do whatever it takes to get a prescription out of him. Borrowing Chris's Land Rover for the mission, I forget that it's a beast of a vehicle and touchy on the gas. Approaching the clinic, my cell phone rings and buzzes simultaneously. Fearing I might miss an important work call, I attempt to answer the phone whilst operating the vehicle.

It lumbers awkwardly, right into another parked car.

Am I even insured?

This minor crash is an indication that medication is not going to help me. I look around and decide to drive away.

March 3, 2010

There's a saying that bad things happen in threes. My preferred explanation for getting booted from the real estate brokerage where I've been killing it in sales. It turns out that the West Vancouver realty crowd is less than welcoming to newcomers in their sandbox.

Disorientated, I have been called into the manager's office. I sit and listen to pleasantries segue into a dismissal. I am being fired. My manager's final words are a hockey analogy. To him I am a player being sent back to the minors after his first year in the National Hockey League. It is not my time. Apparently, this is meant as reassurance that failure now doesn't have to stand in the way of coming back later on to a long and prestigious career. A hockey analogy to fire someone is interesting. Or, in this case, crushing.

Instead of making it known how well I skate, literally in circles around anyone, I'm going to suffer a nervous breakdown for a solid week.

II

HH HH HH HH HH I

"By drowning in alcohol, I am inevitably avoiding tomorrow but not preventing it."

March 10, 2010

Rollerblading around Stanley Park, I take another lap of saviour. I glide on oversized wheels. It's worth mentioning that Travis and Sam helped me move into a new condo.

The studio has a direct view of an overpass and filters glaring sunshine from the east inside. This heats the tiny, dusty fishbowl of a space to a daily melting point. Continuously I exit dressed in a summer wardrobe only to find that the temperature I've perceived from inside these quarters does not match the actual weather. This seems akin to wearing sunglasses even when it's overcast and rainy. Another thing I'm back to. Inappropriately dressed and in shades. Daylight in general still hurts my eyes.

Is it normal for people my age to have ulcers? These conditions represent the state of my nervous system and the best available living arrangements in Downtown Vancouver on short notice.

Since the precise wording on real estate contracts favours the brokerage not me, the shafted agent, everything I have been working for is at risk. My commissions on properties that close in the future will be largely redistributed to other people. So much for buying freedom.

It doesn't cost anything to spend time along the ocean and get some fresh air. Which sounds really healthy except for the fact that anyone passing by along the seawall could get a decent buzz from licking me. My sweat is 40 proof.

Evidence of falling off the proverbial wagon.

If more evidence was required, looking at my new car, at the smashed windshield, provides plenty. This is what happens when you drive intoxicated down an alleyway into a projectile beer bottle.

The cops were there. Immediately. Asking if I wanted to investigate. With blood content in violation of the law, of course I didn't. To hide my intoxication, the door opened just enough to announce that all is well. Doing so I lost my prescription glasses, which I cannot afford to replace. Things can't get much worse.

It seems that putting your personal life on pause, locked away to deal with later, is not actually possible.

Sam offered me legal counsel. Suing is always an option to rectify when we've been wronged. But I don't have the energy for lawyers. I have just enough to focus on something else.

How to be in a healthy relationship with myself. Since I can't find painkillers, I'm back to wanting something else.

March 17, 2010

Not just to check in on his investment but to check in on a friend, Travis is here at my side. As if we lost no time living in different cities, we get along. Walking throughout Downtown we stop for sporadic drinks at patios with alluring lighting, sunlit or artificial. Unofficial bar crawls have always been our speciality. So there's nothing off about this. What's different is that I feel really run down.

Between the second and third patio, I attempt to reinvigorate by taking deep inhales. Yoga breathwork to draw in as much fresh ocean air as my lungs can hold. Exhaling completely, I want to feel like the spring. Fresh and new. A dark spray tan and new suit jacket should help. They don't.

Travis agrees that I should continue to try to look good. It may be my only current asset. I laugh at this but deep inside I know that a youthful appearance is finite. Time, the elements, and certain types of experience age people. By drowning in alcohol, I am inevitably avoiding tomorrow but not preventing it. This is unsettling, yet I order another shot. It arrives and I stare at it. Then, I turn towards Travis.

This breakthrough is interrupted from further down the bar. I hear someone. He is talking to his friend. About me. Dubious. They want to know if I am the White Rabbit.

It dawns on me that they can only be talking about one thing. Reluctantly I walk in their direction and force myself to make direct eye contact with the man talking. The story they are referencing is one I have been avoiding. Partially because I don't want to remember the night in question. By employing selective memory we can hide our faults. Or at least forget them, for a period of time.

I want badly to see this as something serendipitous and give a man named Dallas my number.

The white rabbit evening happened just before the unpopular move-in to Chris's. I had friends over and we proceeded to the back of someone's limousine, from scene to scene, in my case desperately searching for a connection. For something that feels human.

Later, my right eye opened slowly. The terrible taste in my mouth was one I know well. It comes from a body lacking in hydration. A body that has been fed alcohol well beyond what is healthy. I'd thrown up. Maybe late night Chinese food from Tsui

Huang or maybe not. Otherwise, everything was dark. I was not in my own room and not in my own house. There was a cell phone on the night stand. It was mine and the battery was dead.

On the floor directly beside the bed, my clothes. A white fur jacket and white ankle boots. The White Rabbit.

There was no evidence of keys or a purse. Which might explain why I was in a hotel across the street from all the nightclubs.

I refrained from reminiscing about what happened in the wee hours. My hangover wouldn't allow such abstract thinking. Anything beyond placing one foot in front of the other would have been impossible. I left the skanky hotel. In the street, daylight met the jackhammer operating in my head. Garbage overflowed from a dumpster on the corner by Nelson Street. In less than an hour, I had to be at an appointment to drop keys off to a new homeowner. The type of people who have no idea what a drunk I am.

With each step, I made myself feel less disgusting and focused on how to recover keys and get inside my own place.

Professional recovery during another walk of shame. Not the type of housing expertise I make public claim to.

Reminiscing finished.

March 20, 2010

Hiding empty bottles of wine under my sink, I rearrange my things and attempt to arrange my nerves. Dallas is at my door. Then inside my studio.

It's boiling hot.

I open the windows.

We listen to music. I prepare some drinks even though I've had too much already. Everything is hazy. Maybe it's the cigarette smoke. Maybe not. Eventually, Dallas is beside me.

My body cools.

All of a sudden it's freezing.

I look at the wall then a painting. My mind travels to a neutral place where I envision a lake at sunset. I sit on a wooden bench facing this lake and gaze indolently at a thin amber strip of vanishing sunlight.

Beside me, Dallas rests atop salmon-coloured sheets. His skin feels really soft. He's a boy-next-door type. Mid-height. Mid-brown hair. Nice. A safe bet. But he's not sitting on this imaginary bench with me. Lakeside, I'm alone. I begin to question who's going to be by my side at dusk to welcome twilight. I can't relax in intimate company.

March 22, 2010

A lifestyle that ricochets between casual intoxication and warm Yoga doesn't leave much middle ground. My median is Chinatown. It borders the low income housing, abandoned shops, and cracked-out street people that exist along Vancouver's infamous East Hasting strip. To aid in gentrification, new property developments are priced just below Downtown proper. Beyond the eyesore of a small and targeted harsh reality, a block away, people are just as pretentious as anywhere else. These ones just have more tattoos and walk past stores with Mandarin or Cantonese signage out front. Following this path of least resistance, I transferred my real estate license to an office here. My new colleagues are profiting from the neighbourhood's trendiness. Turning right at Tinseltown, I park in front of Dallas's. We're going to watch a movie.

As spectators to someone else's film, just like we can't help but slow down to pass the toothless hookers in front of Save on Meats, we watch to contrast another reality to our own. Or be haunted by it. Or just be. Because even though the choices of how to relate to a movie or the impoverished seem endless, through over exposure, what might have been moving can also become tacit scenery.

Beside Dallas, I close my eyes to everything and kiss his lower lip. My mouth holds on for a long time. He breathes into me and I can feel him. I can feel him move down my throat, my chest, and my legs. My toes point. Like I'm trying to stand on tiptoe. We drift away in time. To a place where I want everything to become nothing. But something prevails.

So after the credits, by the elevator, I convince myself that I won't return here. As hard as I've tried, intimacy isn't giving me what I want it to. No more to see. Yet more to see. No more to feel. Yet more to feel. Uncertainty.

*

March 31, 2010
Shopping.

I drive directly to Yaletown. A neighbourhood famous for miniature dogs and stores to clothe miniature dogs. Inside a boutique I flip through garments hanging on a rail and sigh audibly. The fabric glitters but nothing feels quite like gold.

I go next door and ascend an open stair. A grey powder-coated steel door opens to a second-story hallway. The smell is immediate. Jasmine and bliss. A glass wall and glass door showcase soft lighting and exposed wooden beams. I'm here to buy what I need the most. A six-month Yoga membership.

Wasting no time, I practise. During the entire sixty minutes, I'm here. Present and balanced. A sentiment I want to take with me.

Back on the streets I notice how these buildings are evidence of a neighbourhood that used to be something different. Something other than high-rise condominiums, restaurants with patios, and bourgeoisie shopping. Among it all, I feel exactly like someone who just evaporated into steam. All that was left behind in the studio.

This partially vanished self then goes to sit at a coffee bar and looks down at thousands of pieces. A puzzle. Identified by the telltale ninety-degree angle, I grab a corner piece and slide it in front of me. My strategy is to build the frame. With an outline, it will become easier to piece together the rest. I click together a few more pieces. Looking outside, I see a woman walk by. She holds a large coffee, spilling it slightly to rush towards a man in a fluorescent vest. He's about to slide a long yellow parking ticket under her windshield wiper.

She grabs the violation and enters the driver's side just as a white tow truck blasts by. To hunt for his next prey. As soon as you've been ticketed around here, you're likely to be towed. Even from inside the shop, the sound of that diesel engine is audible. It makes my heart pound. I leave to ensure my own meter's validated.

But first. Just one shop. A pair of Swarovski crystal-studded earrings in the design of a Union Jack invite me inside. As if she can sense my type, the boutique's owner is in front of me handing over silky and soft things. She tells me that she owns every item in three colours. French lace detailing tickles my fingers then disappears into pastel tissue wrapping. The impulse purchases sealed with a scented sticker. I return to my car. Just in time. For a parking ticket.

April 4, 2010

After chatting on the first-floor rooftop patio at Joe Forte's, Sam and I walk to a nearby Holt Renfrew luxury department store. A migratory pattern he could do blindfold.

We're going out this evening to a soirée and want to look smart. New outfits smart. The party is at the home of a married professional couple. Sam's friends. He confessed to me about how excited he is to introduce me to everyone. How he really likes me. I should be satisfied because someone finds me special. Someone who has lovely friends. We're being treated like guests of honour. Sadly, I am dissatisfied. Everyone's shoes and jewelry are much more expensive then my own. This inadequate outfit, not how I do not feel reciprocal endearment for Sam, is what makes me uncomfortable.

Our group travels onward to a mansion in the British Properties and I try to lose my sentiments of inadequacy to the music. This house seems full of respectable party guests. Precisely the illusion that professional catering, lighting, and floral arrangements can create. I walk into another room and wait for a cocktail. There's no use being jealous over other people's possessions. And I should give Sam a chance. Before I finish this pep-talk, grinning wickedly, a man wearing a red windbreaker and running shoes approaches. He's holding a tray of baked chocolate truffles.

I eat three or four. His smile widens. The taste is more truffle than chocolate. Attesting to one ingredient in particular, not customarily used in typical dessert preparation, just in psychedelic confectionaries. Before I can confirm my suspicion, red jacket disappears.

I leave to hide in an upper-floor washroom and welcome hallucination. My reflection is all dilated pupils and an oversized mouth. Children's things adorn the adjacent bedroom. Miniature, cartoon-like, and swirling. Even the simplest surrounding, the wall, is alive with colour and movement.

Accidentally taking mushrooms is not what I need this evening. This causes me to laugh. Uncontrollable and hysterical. This then causes me to cry. A voice in my head, in the tone of someone who has inhaled helium, reminds me that Sam is unlikely to be amused. Moreover, I cannot remember where I've put my new jacket.

I lie on the floor in an attempt to do some mind control. I try a posture called Cobra and lift my chest and rest on my elbows and forearms. Parallel, my forearms become gilded. A head crown drapes beside my face. My hair is snakes. The transformation into an Egyptian statue replica is complete. But I am still as high as Everest. A predicament that causes more tears. They zigzag, like an errant insect. Tickling me. And ruining my make-up.

As a last resort, a cold shower might do wonders.

Unfortunately, in my state, I cannot manage to undress and turn on the water in this child's en-suite washroom. The shower curtain, like a piece of melted cheese, comes off its hooks and curtain pole and wraps itself around my body. Like a burrito. I'm trapped inside the curtain. I am quite stuck, when Sam walks in.

My explanation, that I'm not vandalising the host's home. I've accidently ingested hallucinogens because a man is silently serving magic mushrooms in the form of sweets. It is possible everyone else here is on a nice high. Except for Sam. He is concerned and appalled and manages to peel me out from the conundrum to usher a taxi.

*

April 6, 2010

From the shuttle bus that's about to leave the Lodge at the Four Seasons on Lanai, I don't look any different to the other tourists returning to the sister property at Manele Bay.

Despite the performance at the party, or owing to it, Sam decided that I need more luxurious and secluded pillows to relax my head on. A conclusion I cannot rebut.

In Hawaii, I begin to introduce myself not as a Realtor but as a Yoga Student. One with a lot to learn. Outside the *asanas*, a sense of balance and moderation remains a work in progress.

I've assessed by now that Sam is fifty-five years old and an alcoholic. And not a particularly nice person when he's drunk. This relationship is dead on arrival. A corpse. That is somehow convenient.

After lunch my fork dissects art piece number one: a lemon tart. I look up. Some people's definition of happiness is the perfect balance of sour and sweet, like this tart, prepared to perfection by a pastry chef of distinction.

Sam's definition of happiness, a state I could use an education on, does not include anything sweets-related. His face contorts in disgust. Holding a glass of extra dry white wine, his pinky finger extends towards me. I'm being scolded.

Defiantly, I send the waiter for more. One of everything on the menu. Plates of chocolate tart, carrot cake, and crème brûlée arrive poolside. I indulge in a bit of everything, discard the rest, and observe my surroundings. Giant trees of an ancient orchard, freestanding colonial-style horse stables, and perfectly manicured grass and gardens. Against this backdrop, well-dressed children hunt around for candy-coloured Easter eggs.

Then, I observe myself. Dressed somewhat outlandishly. Eating things rather unsuitable for poolside lounging. With Sam. The sun may kiss my skin but I feel ice cold. Incidentally, something to do with the bottle of wine chilling by our side.

April 8, 2010
Del Mar, the resident masseuse I'm leaving behind on the island, tells me I need more time. The knots in my back are, as he describes, scars.

I sit on the edge of a red clay cliff towering above the bay. It's sunrise. This wonderful hotel and its discriminating guests are down below and far away. Leaving just me, these bluffs, the crashing ocean, and my scar tissue. My legs dangle towards infinity.

My body reclines against a breeze and I close my eyes. Momentarily I am tempted to jump. To leave my soul in Hawaii. Instead I decide to leave bits of what plagues me behind. A partial unload. Throwing stones, I toss my worries into the water. Who knows where they'll go. Sweetheart Rock towers upward, bright rust orange above the lapis lazuli Pacific water. This view radiates a healing energy. Offering an embrace.

It doesn't matter that things will not progress with Sam. He doesn't have bad intentions towards me. On the contrary, he lets me do what I like. He just wants company to travel with.

At night, I've arranged the patio furniture to make a bed under the palm trees. To fall asleep al fresco. Blanketed by the scent of tuberose, I have slept well and listened tirelessly to the ocean in the background. The sound of crashing waves. This sound, now, is inside me.

To be here is a gift. I feel safe. Peaceful. I can feel what it's like to relax. There's a dark green glass bottle. Inside, I discover a folded square of paper. Someone else's poetry. Subtly, I feel differently than I used to. I produce a pen and write a response on the flipside. Sending this modified message out to sea.

What feels like happiness, is this very moment. A moment that only took 4,743 miles and a five-star hotel to arrive at.

IO

||||| ||||| ||||| ||||| ||||| |

*"Sight can magnify faults or showcase splendour.
Which you focus on, is a choice."*

April 10, 2010

Recently, the owner of the salon where I get my hair done (sparingly, given how humid it is – perpetually blown hair would be impossible) wanted to set me up with another client of the salon. Who happens to be the most eligible player on the Vancouver Canucks. This sport is revered, the professional athletes are gods. Neither of which I particularity worship. Is it a good idea to date someone else right now? An athlete, I decide, will sport an athletic body. One that might be nice to play with. I'm feeling rather playful following my last vacation. So I take the number and waste little time to set up a meeting.

The Canuck invites me to a local pub. This isn't a date because he's in there with seven mates. I opt to wear my highest heels, leather leggings, sequins, a full set of glam eyelash extensions, and a push up bra (that adds two cup sizes), but all very casually. This is a pub, and not a date, after all. Hockey star's haircut is shorter than I imagined but his thighs are deliciously thick. As if they might tear through regular-fitting jeans. I sit down beside him. Chat, flirt, and assess whether we have chemistry.

He wants me to go watch him play hockey. I have friends who will jump at gratuitous tickets. Momentarily I wonder if I should disclose anything. How I've been traumatized by rape. How my last boyfriend and I had quite an unhealthy relationship. How lately I've been accompanying Sam.

The thing is, there's no way to bring these things up.

April 15, 2010

The roar is monumental. Typical of an NHL playoff. Everything is buzzing.

I take some of it in then abruptly announce to my girlfriend that I want to leave.

Parked in a former client's parking lot across the street, my car waits. The last remaining perk of real estate, other people's parking.

Stopping and going, I swerve to avoid the flood of post-hockey pedestrians. Following Pacific, a road that encompasses Downtown, I turn left into an alley. My parking garage opens slowly. I descend the ramp and turn into the first available stall too quickly at the wrong angle and hit a concrete pillar.

The back door is now adorned with a jagged dent.

I decide that this isn't a good sign. Then exit the car park and re-park in the street. Out in the open.

April 17, 2010

The dogs' tiny feet move noiselessly through the lobby. I can feel the concierge smiling. Not at me but at them.

Inside the elevator, we stand on a mat that's changed each day to correspond with the day of the week. The letters spell Saturday. I begin to wonder if they'll change it to Sunday precisely at midnight. Otherwise, everything around me is beige. Not washed-out beige but golden beige. Hotel beige. The shade inside the Pan Pacific.

The door to the suite opens. Greeting me, DP. He looks the

same as he used to and wastes no time presenting his suite. I follow politely, responding in agreement, pretending to be impressed by the balconies and the sweeping views. He is as if hanging out with an old friend. I'm here so that I can leave and be able to repair my car and more. The timing of his proposition, to fool around for payment, just like old times, seems opportune.

Without further deliberation, I attack him. Like a hurricane might. I expose my silhouette, sheerly covered in a full-body catsuit. Scratching at the lace, I slowly rip it off into shreds. Then, I take pieces of the fabric and tie his arms. Then, around his throat I wrap black nylon. Then, I fill his mouth.

Like I'm the one without oxygen, I disconnect from the scene playing out. Momentarily, this suppresses all of my other concerns. About how I perhaps shouldn't be here. Straddling him, I begin to hate myself for doing this. And slap him hard.

The rest of the date seems to proceed without any emotion on my part. I just have to act in a way that was memorized in a previous epoch. My concern fades. To sexual climax.

Afterwards, just as I came, I leave. Through the lobby.

The night looks different by now. The expansive mountain range to the north is illuminated by distant lights reflecting in the ocean. I roll down the window to hurl the shredded remains of the catsuit out. Littered into the street, my past with DP is left in Coal Harbour to die a secret. I'm never going to be with him ever again. The streets are empty and I arrive to my place in silence.

May 2, 2010
Despite all the Yoga classes, a sense of harmony isn't arriving.

May 3, 2010
Along a crescent street that's situated between the seawall and a

marina, I pass the Roundhouse. My favourite for coffee and sushi. At the neighbouring address lives the Canuck. This location is unaffordable to ninety-nine per cent of the population and, also, one of my favourites. I'm only thinking about the property, not about how to have a nice date with someone who I may be quite well suited to.

Inside, my first observation is SportsCenter on TV. Second, his walking cast. This is the real reason we're on a date. He has some time off to heal an injury. I'm not so hungry for food. Nor do I want to further injure his million-dollar leg.

In an attempt to find more muted lighting, I head to the stairwell. And begin to kiss him. I think that seeing DP the other day has rendered me in a certain mode. Fast and evocative. I can sense how excited he is and lower his trousers to perform an exceptional, but quick, blow job. Exceptionally quick. The speed within which this has occurred is embarrassing. No articles of my own clothing have been removed. It dawns on me to keep him sitting on the stairs, so I swing my thigh over to straddle him. On top I can achieve the pleasure I so desire. In my mind a rather disturbing train of thought persists.

Hockey.

Ice skating.

Arenas.

Just more things that have broken me.

Figure skating. By high school I went every day, sometimes twice a day. At 5:45 am and 3:45 pm. In terms of power, stamina, and overall movement, I've become a master. But each time I grew, even a quarter-inch, my centre of gravity would shift. I don't like to remember falling. Again and again and again. The part of my jaw that I broke skating begins to ache. I shift how I'm sitting to conceal my deformed feet.

The thought train chugs on. Figure skating competitions. I

was the girl who never won. That feeling, of always being in the bottom half, returns. Performance anxiety and a sense of failure. Is this where I learned to be masochistic? No. I cannot do a hockey player. Instead, I excuse myself, go home, and delete his number.

This is not how to successfully go on a date.

*

May 8, 2010

Soft wind passes over and under the tallest bridge in the city. Rooftops and ocean span the horizon. Lyrics play. The world is telling me to stop getting high off my own supply.

These words linger. Through Yoga I am learning that we all have vital energy. It exists in all of us and has nothing to do with the food we eat or the oxygen we breathe.

It is something more universal.

Most people can and do exist with such little quantities of this *prana* that they simply get by, day to day, not actually living in awareness, but not dead either. It dawns on me that disconnect happens when our vital energy is dangerously low.

May 10, 2010

With new understanding, at another doorway I arrive. Curiosity to proceed is a trait, like readiness, that some people can sense. One of my new real estate colleagues, Claire, is this type of person. She sees me arrive at the threshold and begins to wave her hand, motioning to walk forward. From her mouth, soft words.

There is no suffering.

I take a cautious step and want to argue that suffering exists. The proof, that I've felt it. That I see it all around. Especially in Eastside Vancouver. I don't rebut though. I step through the opening and don't look back. Ahead, a gate that leads to a garden.

Claire's words linger in this space. The next transformation is that I believe her. There is no more suffering.

May 11, 2010

My horoscope indicates that the mind's thoughts are a preview of life's attractions. An ode to Einstein and also an introduction to the power of manifestation. To visualize exactly what we want is a method to begin making it a reality.

I am what I think I am.

June 18, 2010

This whole manifestation thing is easier if you have a concise vision of what you want. As someone routinely disillusioned by what I think I want, the outcome is still very confusing.

At the Mexican-themed birthday party for Barby, now a yummy mummy with a fiancé in tow, I scheduled a rendezvous with Robert, who's piercing blue irises retain some sort of hold over me. Even though it's been three years since we last laid eyes on each other, he wastes no time to impart that my biggest flaw is how I'm rude. Before I can comment on this, the guy sat beside us on a bench outside the Ship and Anchor pub literally tears off his denim pants to remodel them into shorts.

Maybe I am rude. It's going to be a process to develop more poise. Moderation wasn't available for me to grab from thin air. To start a new beginning, you must start. Somewhere. Perhaps by finishing an old cycle or by leaving it behind. If the guy at the pub can so swiftly refashion his jeans, with such little effort or concern for the original garment, it follows that with more time I can erase the tiny vice Robert speaks of. I can also do with company who has something nice to say.

*

June 27, 2010

My Brazilian blown-out hair billows silkily. I lay atop a white chaise that matches my white bikini at the Thompson Hotel in Los Angeles. The evening sun blankets my face casting a reassuring sentiment. Someone I want as a client is here with me. We are to attend a party being sponsored by someone else that I want as a client. So I tell myself this is a work trip.

Upon arrival we went directly to the most luxurious spa around. One facial and full body massage later, I am ready for tonight's party and sip champagne poolside in anticipation. LA is smiling and fish scale tiles around the pool sparkle like jewelry. The water ripples from small waves created by the embrace of a lone couple, together in the deep end.

For someone curious about the next steps along a spiritual path, partying amongst semi-nude painted playmates, and men who paid far too much to be partying amongst semi-nude painted playmates, may seem incompatible.

It's not entirely.

I place a small diamond-shaped pill in my mouth. These pills, salt enzymes, my travel companion tells me are custom made. Some sort of private experimental medicine developed by a neurologist who works for the American military. I find the story fascinating. The truth is, I have no idea what these pills are. Whatever it is, the outcome is mildly stimulating, mildly euphoric, and mildly amazing. We go to the Playboy Mansion and all evening I do not feel the need for even a drop of booze. Just some water.

This party is teeming with people. When my eyes close I think about Claire. So full of advice. Her hand is close to mine. Her eyes look at me with connection and understanding. She leans in, with interest, to ask a series of questions about what I want. Her focus is on relationships. With men. All of them.

The emptiness in whatever I respond with to Claire is telltale. She wants to know how I'm going about life to meet a partner who cares about my heart. The truth is, I'm not. I am in LA with someone I have been trying to sell a million-dollar apartment with a view to. The truth is, he will one day buy such an apartment. Immediately, however, he just wants to hang out and do fun things. I could be working with other people. As part of a team now, there are endless leads and many listed properties to sell. But searching for immediate gratification as well, I am someone who mostly avoids going to work and is very interested in having fun in Los Angeles.

Time will continue to go by. I may simply have to go along with it.

At the party, my heart beats slower than the music. I extend my hand and pick up a paintbrush to dip into turquoise iridescent paint, speckled with silver. This colour refracts sunlight against my tanned skin. I paint a picture on my stomach about what I value: family. I'm not always on the best terms with all of mine, but I still value family above anything else. This artwork, I will continue to envision. Like a badge someone earns after an unearthing chat with someone like Claire. I will wear it like armour, to protect myself from bad habits and guide myself toward the future.

I will not play the game where I fantasize that someone I've just met stands the chance of miraculously healing me or transforming my pain into something different. I look down at what I've painted. An image of patience dancing around LA until sunrise.

*

July 18, 2010
Today's date isn't actually July 18. That just happens to be

187

the expiry date on some sour cream I'm using to accompany something I bought at 7-Eleven and shouldn't be eating. These junk-food meals have serious repercussions. Mainly indigestion. Eating like this leaves me feeling the opposite of pretty, content, motivated, or proud, yet I devour the irresponsible food.

My eyelashes are thin and broken. A technician advised rehab. It seems that taking a break has both macroscopic and microscopic applications.

Eyelash rehab takes up to six months. So does small intestinal rehab.

Lately I have an acute inability to sleep. Insomnia I blame on a current heat wave. At sundown, unable to sleep, I walk the seawall looking for the moon. Looking for anything, really. I walk onward. Footsteps tap away at my animosities. On an energy level, even with all the physical Yoga, I'm still totally lost.

I want nothing more than to be found. By someone reaching out to hold my hand. But it's been so long since anyone held mine for the right reasons. I can't even remember what it feels like.

July 20, 2010

Unannounced, Sam pulled up in a taxi headed to the airport. He shared that his father just passed away and wants to know if I will go with him to Calgary for the funeral. Ideally his company at such a delicate time would be someone capable of dealing with such a huge loss in a tasteful manner.

People who experience death need a hug, condolence, or empathy. Preferably all three. Not an extortionist demanding things from the Chanel boutique before sullying your bed at the hotel room with another man.

Again, I should stop taking off and focus on selling properties. Yet again I prioritise getting away from binge eating and feeling gross. And this time my mood will improve. Not only have I decided to spontaneously accompany Sam on the trip, but I have also decided to call someone as soon as the plane's wheels touch down. Someone, aka Robert.

Robert and I passed Sam in the lobby on the way to Sam's hotel room. I said something about needing twenty minutes. The resulting scenario, twenty minutes later, could be regarded as comical. Sam entered, to prepare a cocktail. He offered one to me and another to Robert, then continued to act like the whole ordeal was rather normal. Robert got uncomfortable and left. Sam asked if I at least knew who he was. Instead of getting into it, I claimed we met in the street.

Then, Sam checked out of the hotel. We did not fly back to Vancouver together.

*

July 24, 2010

I finally made an appointment to have laser eye surgery. I'm unsure why it took me so long, but things are finally going to be different.

Sight can magnify faults or showcase splendour. Which you focus on, is a choice.

There's no way to assess the opportunities we have missed due to not being able to see them. Someone once told me that in sports you can't count past goals, only today's game. So, my focus isn't on the things I didn't see before but on what I can see now. Specifically, an expansive marina and the interior of a float plane. My girlfriend from university and I are flying to Salt Spring Island.

From around an ear muffler, the fluffy white hair of the senior citizen sitting in front of us reflects the sun, the plane's aluminum cladding, and the water below. It glows. The plane's propeller starts and loudly cuts into the ocean. Like a chainsaw. We become a boat. Then the water sprays around us, and we lift out of the water in flight. Becoming a flying machine. An airplane. The dock below begins to dwarf in size. Coal Harbour becomes smaller and smaller. From the air, this eagle-eye view reveals a vast peninsula of densely forested islands that pepper the Gulf Coast. I see all of this through my new eyes, shielded by even newer sunglasses. Even with the limited vision of post-operative eyes, I can see more than ever before.

A red MINI Cooper is waiting for us, like a smiling cherry, at the dock. I hug our host warmly. Someone I met passing through the airport alone the other day. I told him briefly about the Robert-in-Sam's-hotel-room scandal. About how awful I felt. His response, that to feel pretty is to add value to the world. Salt Spring, he says, can erase the ugly. It's likely that he is correct. Foremost, because his home and gardens are stunning. Luxurious. Unique. Artisan. Their energy attracts butterflies. This is a sanctuary.

Each room is decorated with love and impeccable taste. Bright silks hang suspended from a vaulted ceiling. A mix of antique, import, and modern furniture complement one another in interior success. Bottles of water embellished with crystals line the open bar. Flowers, each larger and brighter than the next, grow throughout the rolling landscape, past heirloom chickens and unique orbs and sculptures. A path zigzags down a hill. Like a spice trail, leading to the rich orient in the distance. The lake. An emerald city. This weekend we are Moroccan Dorothy. Off to see the Wizard.

Over dinner we discuss fortune telling, and the host suggests we summon the local tea leaf reader. She is regarded as one of the best. My soup-bowl glass of bordeaux agrees. A psychic reading is a good call.

When the woman arrives I get to visit her first. At the formal dinner table she reads my leaves. Her words float into the air and I can see her face through them, but the letters themselves are blurry. I look far away outside towards the lake, unable to hear her. When we don't want to hear something, we don't. She's not uttering the words I want to hear. Nothing about a fairy tale ending. There's nothing about true Love in her prediction whatsoever.

Instead of concluding that I'm looking too far ahead, I drink more wine, breathe in, and accept that the tea leaf reader is telling me my future.

My immediate destiny is to share a message: unconventional women are not demons. My eyes began to water as I refill the red soup cup. All women have a right to their own bodies. To their own pleasures. She finishes by saying that the next chapter will begin in a coffee shop. Somewhere foreign. Somewhere outside Canada.

9

卌 卌 卌 卌 卌 ||

"What am I doing to ensure that I meet someone who falls in love with my heart?"

August 3, 2010

Curled up to relax with a novel, I wait in the lobby for Barby to arrive. Some holidays are to unwind. This one feels a date with destiny. First, to see the difference that time can make. It has been exactly four years since my last visit to Miami.

People assume that we are Brazilian and that we are sisters. Poolside, like a tropical display of samba and laughter, we allow this misinterpretation. The attention is intoxicating. If people opened their eyes, our slight red sunburns would hint at the truth.

August 7, 2010

I should put the more vulnerable pieces of myself beside Barby's Harry Winston engagement ring, secure in the hotel safety deposit box. A Miami trip would be more practical that way. She doesn't want to lose her most valued jewelry. And I'm just prone to getting lost.

We let South Beach style rapidly turn to no panties and no consequences. Dance music, lots of bling, matching costumes, professional athletes, Sheikhs, designer sunglasses, and oiled skin abound. By now an apple, a bottle of vodka, another of tequila, some coffee, three pieces of sashimi, and seven almonds are the cornerstones of our diet. The words of Claire still echo in my ear. Very faintly.

What am I doing to ensure that I meet someone who falls in love with my heart?

I decide to go on a mission to find out. Starting at the party next door at the W Hotel's pool.

August 8, 2010

I ignore Claire's attempt to steer me in a better direction and opt to play the game with someone I've just met. The game being me telling myself that our encounter is fate. I am bewitched by the chemistry.

This person happens to be a man I met beside the dancefloor, where I was swaying as casually as one does after five days and twelve hours of non-stop drinking in the sun. Sensually swaying. He was nearby, at the bar, looming above my head. As one does at six foot four.

We danced. Nothing needed to be said, really. Our bodies did the talking. The game starts when I ask him if he wants to get married. Not a conventional pick-up line but straight to the point. He said why not, so we browse the lobby's boutique to select a dress and an engagement ring. Green silk with black feather sleeves to go with a light green stone set in gold, surrounded by crystals.

To a suite at the Standard Hotel across the bay and away from South Beach, we head to consummate the proposal. The pool is breathtaking. I can't figure out how to get down to it so descend, as one might, by climbing down the awning. My new husband for the night meets me at the lower level deck. Then, we jump in. The water greets us with a splash. Enveloping our bodies.

His eye are clear like the pool with a crystal glow. More icy than my ring. And more beautiful.

We go to a room and through the night let the best sensation

I know fill it. This overcomes my body and I feel paralysed by it. Pain and longing and vulnerability and need and excitement, all at once. My current drug of choice: the one night stand.

August 9, 2010

This morning is when I speak to my faux-husband for the first time. He's asks what I'm running away from. From nothing, I lie. He doesn't respond. Then, like it was just a dream, we part ways.

Even though it's just a game, the high of last night quickly fades and I feel rather sad. Holding my breath, I text him. A few hours later, he's back. To take me for dinner. We sit side by side on clear resin chairs. The tables have white tablecloths and the room is mostly black with red velvet decorations. This all matches the glasses of wine that separate us.

I learn that he likes triathlons. That his real age is younger than I thought. That he is married. For real. To another women. And that his children, aged two and four, are at home with his wife.

He's right about me playing games because I'm running away from something. And so is he.

After not eating, a limo carries us off into the night. I'm tired. A disco ball spins in front of my eyes. Nearby, inside an egg-shaped chair, suspended from the ceiling by a chain, Barby, wearing a red skin-tight bandage dress, spins too. Several semi-nude anorexic go-go dancers spin behind here. They all turn in unison. I am dizzy from it all. So I close my eyes and stop looking.

I don't know where the strength comes from but my feet carry me from the club to the hotel room. Barby is in the bed beside me. She's sleeping soundly.

Draping my arm across my body, my fingertips tuck underneath a bandage to explore the slightly raised outline of a heart. The one etched in black, tattooed on my ribs.

A permanent reminder. This is not a love story.

*

August 10, 2010

I got back home to an intriguing email. It is from someone who bought me coffee in Miami. I am being invited to Colombia, South America. Apparently, I'll like it there.

I hit Facebook to investigate the sender. Claire's voice, whispering so quietly now I can barely hear it, asks whether this man will care about my heart. Meanwhile, Facebook reveals two men listed in the same city with the same name.

Profile photo number one, a scanned vintage deal, depicts a man on a polo horse. The out-of-focus image plus polo helmet obscure his facial features. The second profile photo, also faceless, is a baklava-wearing man, crouched in the jungle. Gun in one hand and fanned display of money in the other.

I send two friend requests.

*

August 12, 2010

I received a parcel today. A late birthday present from Barby. It's a guide on how to shop for a husband. I give the author, who seems to think that finding a husband is akin to finding a well-fitting and appropriate black dress, some credit. Part of me hates the analogy. Another part of me is worried. Instead of basically everything I've been doing, it appears that I should have been focusing on marriage. Commitment.

But are most marriages these days even about commitment? The marriage contract seems to me just that. A contract. Like the kind we enter into with our bank, landlord, auto dealership, or employer. Just like I feel uncertain about those types of contracts, I am not a solid candidate to enter into one of matrimonial

195

proportions just yet either. Though an island off Istanbul in an ancient coliseum would be nice for a wedding. As would a dress by Oscar de la Renta.

I flip through more pages of the book. Similar to Claire's advice, it suggests to make a list. If a man fits my basic criteria, I'm allowed to date him. When two different forces suggest the same thing, one might as well give it a try. In this case, a preordained list about my future husband. Out comes a pen.

I struggle to write.

August 14, 2010

The Internet is the number one place to market for anything. So if I'm going to shop for a husband, I might as well use it.

I fill out a profile for an online dating site. Within three minutes, twenty emails arrive. An automated response of sorts explains that I take coffee each day at JJ Bean. Mr. Online Enquirer, all twenty of them, is free to stop in and make an introduction.

This is my version of speed dating.

August 23, 2010

It was Coco Chanel who said that in order to be irreplaceable one must always be different. On the contrary, underwhelmingly, everyone seems rather the same. How boring.

I've met some Asians and some Caucasians. Men who are skinny and those who are portly. Short to tall. With and without hair. Beyond the physical, we all seem pretty much the same. Stuff about jobs. Hobbies. Being nice.

The husband shopping guide indicates I should focus on Nice.

September 15, 2010

We wear very little, in terms of clothing. We bend over. Lunge.

Spread. Tight black fabric stretches in a way to expose more than the contours of a panty line. It's graphic. Bodies, dripping with sweat. A steamy vapour fragranced subtly with lemongrass forms a universal dew. To deepen the positions today we're using one another's body weight. Someone else's legs are intertwined with mine. Her feet walk along my calves in a Thai Yoga massage.

Partner Yoga has me beginning to pay attention to who else is practising Yoga. Maybe here is where I can meet someone special.

For a long time I practised with my eyes closed the entire class. This helps you look inward. And helps you not critique your own body.

With my eyes closed, I envision *samadhi*. A state of intense concentration achieved through meditation. Then I open my eyes. They lock onto a man in the back of the room. I bend over further to check him out from between my legs, upside down.

Hanging out by the tea service after class, a swarm of gorgeous people sip invitations to explore this Yoga community more intimately.

*

September 16, 2010

Another email arrives from the Colombian. Alejandro. The polo player, it turns out. Though he also has guns in the jungles of Colombia. They're just not overtly pictured on Facebook. The correspondence had me at horses. Which he thinks I will like. Travelling to South America beats the winter here. A season upcoming that I'm keen to avoid.

*

September 17, 2010

From beside a wooden beam in the dimly-lit room, a man approaches me. Squatting down beside my mat, I can feel warmth and can see every hair on his body. Slick with sweat and clinging onto a damp chest. Based on his tan, I assume he takes frequent vacations.

He asks me to dinner. Which I agree to. Over the course of our meal, as he speaks, I begin to recognise him. Not from previous classes but from when I asked him for a job a few years ago. This man, a commercial realtor, is also friends with Travis.

With cautious precision, I laugh over how we met prior to forward bend. His face winces. He looks in shock because he's married. Both the explanation for why he didn't offer me a job, and also for why we shouldn't be on a date right now.

Apparently his wife would kill him.

It turns out that by trying to follow Barby's book, I'm shopping all right. For everyone else's husband.

October 2, 2010

Yoga can be very sensual. I like to move as if I'm making love.

This all seems very healing up until the dead of night. Nights that remain sleepless. Even though I'm trying so hard. I feel, frankly, fried.

Just like how the lungs of a dead smoker are black, if there was a way to inspect my insides, you would see that they, too, are eerily dark.

October 10, 2010

The dull grey light makes for great photographs, but I find it blinding. More so than direct sunlight. Bare legs look old and garish against the asphalt sidewalk. My coat is long enough to cover the heinous mini dress underneath, but nothing can cover my face. Marred by scratches. Indicative of a bad fall.

Last night I slipped.

It would be convenient to blame a full moon. Like how in fables werewolves emerge, so does this ravenous wolverine.

What felt like flying last night feels the opposite today.

All the human energy I have is spent. What walks down the sidewalk is an empty vessel. I cringe to think about the unravelling.

No one's returning my panicked calls or texts. Likely, the rest of the world is sleeping. Maybe, no one cares. Back at my condo, I stare at a large bag of potato chips. The Yoga mat, rolled and propped against the coffee table, stares back. I place the shoes I wore to walk home in the garbage. Those disgusting high heels.

I can't remember if I planned any sort of work today. It doesn't matter. My knees bend, lowering my thighs and pelvis towards the floor. Crouched, my upper body falls sideways. Here, I lay. Curled in a fetal position. Beside dog poop. Two accidents on the floor.

October 25, 2010

It's 5 am and my car window is smashed in. Either for the marked real estate keys on the console or the muffins on the passenger seat. It's been exactly four days since I last slept. A lingering unease indicates that I narrowly missed the assailant.

Exhausted, I go to Sam's to drink wine, watch movies, and order enough sushi takeout for seven people. On the way out I take his new sunglasses. The best in polarized lens technology makes the flat grey sky even flatter. And a shade more grey. Looking at nothing and everything, in a kind of meditation, I drive away. Directionless.

Broken shards of glass flake onto the seat beside me. I ponder what would happen if I ate some. Would it cut my insides? This so-called temple that I've become hyper aware of?

I keep driving. Around and about are people with strollers. People with dogs. People with family, with friends. None of them look on the verge of breakdown. I stop and park in front of a department store and contemplate spending the money Sam gave me on couture instead of car repair. I exit and walk up to the window. My palms press against the glass. In the reflection, I see a face.

Someone so desperate.

*

October 26, 2010

Facing Abbott Street, I sit at one of the frosted-glass desks of this modern office. An oversized panoramic image of Downtown stands out against the painted white concrete interior. Her waist-length jet black hair and calculating eyes meet mine. It's Danli. A woman I've been showing property to. I stand so she can see me.

In walks a Chinese man behind her. At the key cupboard a colleague is fumbling around. The sound of metal jingles. They're here to pick up keys for two properties she's just closed on. Properties that I showed her but for which the man accompanying her wrote the purchase contracts. They were submitted directly to the office behind my back, excluding my name.

Instead of explaining the situation and asking for an introduction fee, I just say congratulations. In real estate we are not paid for working, but for contracts and closings. A reality I accepted long ago.

The entrance mirror reflects a multi-coloured Louis Vuitton monogram bag, clutched by her side. She leaves. The door shuts, until I press on it to head out myself.

I have no desire to work another day in this industry. Might as well stop pretending otherwise.

8

||||| ||||| ||||| ||||| ||||| ||

*"Language can't always explain where you've been.
The eyes, however, can."*

November 10, 2010

Unsurprisingly, to pass through US customs en route to Bogotá, Colombia, is a hassle. Thankfully, I have ample time. Three additional security checks and one detention later, and I'm on the final flight. It dawned on me how badly I need to escape. This aircraft could equally well be flying to Siberia, Afghanistan, or the Ivory Coast. The list of invitations I'd have accepted includes anywhere that wasn't where I woke up.

To escape what keeps you up at night is not to run into the arms of Latin America. But for some reason I don't keep that sentiment in the forefront of my mind. This plane is heading towards the unknown. To be immersed in a different world and to see things from a new angle is to learn how to break the vicious cycle of being stuck in a vicious cycle.

From the mindset of nothingness, everything is possible.

November 12, 2010

I arrived in the morning of a new time zone. The guy here to pick me up is not married. He is single. In addition to owning horses at a ranch, this is what I like about him. Facts confirmed through one of seven emails we exchanged, and the total extent of what I know about this man and his country.

We originally met in Café Bustelo, the coffee shop adjoined to the Gansevoort Hotel lobby, in Miami. Barby and I had stopped in for espresso, sashimi, and water. Critical implements in South Beach that particular morning. When I went to pay for the nourishment it had been taken care of by the figure sitting at the small table closest to the front window. Whether or not he expected a thank you, I thanked him anyway.

He asked if I wanted anything else. I did. Some chocolate. The bar caught my eye not because I wanted sweets but because the packaging stood out. A large red heart set against mellow yellow.

A few days later I spotted him again near a valet stand. So I reached into my purse to flash him the chocolate bar. Miami sign language. I then gave him the single business card I had brought along.

Alejandro is wearing track pants and waiting at the airport. His stance, wide-legged and confident, is characteristic of vague familiarity. Aside from this detail, we're meeting up for the first time.

Flying across the world for a first date seems perfectly normal.

In the vehicle, Alejandro changes the music from reggaeton to something else. A ballad. *Vallenato*. It gives way to another piece. The type of harmony to inspire social dancing. *Bachata*. I understand no lyrics, but the rhythms rocks my soul.

We're driving to a ranch in the countryside. His vehicle races along the highway in the city outskirts. A city that sprawls. Dirty brick buildings covered in graffiti mark the periphery of the busy highway. At ground level are shops that sell tires and snacks. Between us and these buildings are people. Everywhere there are people. In a city of millions, people exist in cars and trucks, on motorcycles and busses. Some are on foot, walking, and others are riding bikes. Some are with kids. I pay close attention to those who pull their T-shirt over their mouth to buffer breathing in thick diesel air. I observe all of these people and wonder what they do. We pass people who seem to be content wearing a thick layer of black exhaust. One of them is pulling a handmade wooden trailer. It's filled with cardboard and wooden scraps. We pass by his donkey. A Colombian recycling program, Alejandro tells me. The country flooded badly last week. Even if it's a bit swampy and murky in places, I decide that these surroundings are beautiful. Exactly as they are.

It's become evident that this Toyota FJ cruiser, a brilliant blue jay colour, is more tank-like than its counterpart in North America would be. An attribute of any vehicle armoured to repel bullets. Some of the other vehicles we pass have this quality. But most do not. At sunset, I listen to Alejandro explain a brief history about rebels and kidnappings, two things that used to prevail. Essentially, the Colombian Guerrillas began as a group of people who did not agree with how the country's land was being used. Whatever this movement has evolved to is uncertain. He explains that the doors of the truck shall remain locked and the windows up. Unless he tells me otherwise, I have nothing to worry about.

We eventually turn left off the highway onto a narrow dirt road. A man who works inside a small concrete building runs to the gate and waves the blue bird past. The guard. Now on a secondary dirt road, Alejandro rolls down the windows. It's dark now and our music drifts from the stereo into wide open space. I can smell a damp scent. Bog-like. We drive in a direction of no lights. Beyond the melodies is the crunching sound of tires on gravel road, barking dogs, and tree leaves rustling in the distance.

Eventually we reach the ranch house. I exit the car. A rubber boot-wearing man comes to carry my bags. I follow him and

Alejandro through double hand-cut wooden doors that lead into a huge foyer. The suitcases are carried further down the main-floor hallway to one of the bedrooms. Beyond the entrance is a massive formal sitting area. Everything is grand, antique, and durable. The floors and furniture and lighting are made from thick stone, cushioned leathers, wool, cast iron, and exotic wood. His father collected significant art from the Orient. I gaze upwards at the coffered ceiling and decide, I love it here. Shedding my footwear I sit down on a Persian rug in front of a wood-burning fireplace. It's bigger than most walk-in closets. I close my eyes and remind myself that I am in Colombia. How relaxing.

A woman, also wearing rubber boots, arrives to prepare a fire. I help her because I want to do it myself. Be the firestarter. The grandiose flames lick at the air. A log crackles, splitting the silence. My entire body is warm.

Tiny shadows dance across Alejandro's face. He's sitting beside me and I'm looking right at him. I can see everything about him. Between us, a green box. Aguardiente. A clear Colombian spirit. I grab the box to sip the pungent liquid and smile, deciding here and now that I trust these new people. Conversation is irrelevant because I trust them all, without question. Here in front of a fire, in rural Colombia, I decide to trust everything around me. Completely.

After the night cap, I go to the room my things have been unpacked in. At a sprawling Colombian ranch, finally, I sleep. Soundly.

November 13, 2010

The sun rose to illuminate a vast surrounding of green. Old manors, cattle, horses, dogs, and magnificent bushes decorated with bright fuchsia flowers. Fields rimmed by hand-built fences, trees taller than the sky, and red dirt roads extend around the ranch. The air smells different here. Not like a farm. But like Colombia.

The workers are breeding a horse. An activity that requires human intervention. I stand under some trees to watch the female horse being led into the pen by another man in rubber boots. The stallion awaits. Above me, the sky is turning grey and dark clouds roll in. The men lead the horses towards one another. It begins to rain. Thunder booms and lightning flashes through the trees and across the world. The energy of this moment shrinks me. I look down to my right, at a small Colombian boy who is looking back at me. He karate chops my leg then retreats to hiding behind a tree trunk. Alejandro is at my other side. I reach my hand to his. We hold hands in the rain.

November 14, 2010

There are innumerable horses but I'm straddling Alejandro's selection. A dirty white mare. Her name is Sapo. The reins fall loosely towards her neck because I trust everything, including the horse, and ride her casually. We trot to a pen. Inside is a light brown foal. Alejandro asks me to pick a name, so I select Zahir. Visible, present, and incapable of going unnoticed.

We reach a polo field and Sapo ambles slightly towards the wooden ball that Alejandro is hitting down the field. I watch him do this and listen to instructions on how to replicate the motion. With my own mallet in hand, Sapo canters to the ball. Legs clutch horse and upper body twists. Right arm extends back. Hinge at the waist and dip to lower. Connect mallet head with ball.

Clink.

The sound of polo.

*

November 19, 2010

Colombian cocaine is nowhere on my agenda. At least, not processed cocaine. Crouched down, squatting in a hut with several natives in the Amazon rainforest, I'm forced to decide where to draw the line on this. They're stirring a concoction and explaining the Shamanic tradition of taking Ayahuasca, a psychedelic drug. Locally, it's called Yagé, pronounced Yah-Hey. This spiritual tradition, an important ritual amongst these people, facilitates the journey to becoming an adult. Even though none of them speak any English, this story is clear in their eyes. English, Spanish, or Portuguese, it doesn't matter. Language can't always explain where you've been. The eyes, however, can.

Alejandro, ever mischievous, looks to me and asks whether I want some Yagé. I say no. Thank you. I don't need to be tripping out in the Colombian rainforest. The ship for intensive psychedelics sailed on me long ago. However, the green paste everyone seems to be sucking on looks permissible. This is a paste of coca leaf, to chew and suck on. Aside from this, Colombian cocaine is not on my agenda. Alternatively, I am starting to be high on something else. High on Life.

To relax, a word the guide seems concerned about, I drink yellow cans of Anguilla beer. He bought a stockpile of it and offers me one any time the energy intensifies. It's an effective regime. Clearly, if I'd had permanent access to the wonders of the Amazon and a beer-wielding Sherpa, it's safe to say that life to date would have been rather different.

After the visit with the natives, we travel onwards. To somewhere between Leticia and tourist-accessible rainforest. Tonight's sleeping quarters are some that could be described as rustic. Basically, we're staying in a hut.

Someone brings me dinner. Something that's wrapped in a leaf. It's spicy and delicious. A million little bugs crawl in a never-ending row along the table. I look up at the thatched ceiling. Perched on a rafter is a pet bird. I decide to press into a handstand against a beam and bend my legs to leverage them towards my head. This position, called Scorpion, makes me feel alive. It's not the coca paste. It's vital energy.

November 20, 2010

Grenades and screaming wake us. Sounds I'm not accustomed to. Ruckus and explosion. My reflex is not to panic. Instead, I roll over and return to sleep. Alejandro goes to investigate. No matter what happens in Colombia, sleep is my priority.

It turns out that a state military camp is located nearby. Hence the bombs and kafuffle.

I have no idea who these soldiers are practising to fight. I pass by some of them. Presumably on a training hike, these young men look parched and exhausted. In comparison, I'm brimming. A smile as wide as an oversized sun hat, my main accessory.

In the Amazon, the sole intense battle I can see is internal. In one corner, the need for a schedule and activities. In the other, complete acceptance of everything.

The opponent, desire for planning, wages a brilliant campaign. She demands that we set out into the jungle for our own intensive multi-day hike.

Our guide, paid to accommodate demands coming from me, summoned an adolescent of the jungle to take us on the journey. Walking behind him, I watch how the young man moves. Through dense terrain, he places one foot in front of the other. No special techniques to avoid a branch or a puddle. Just even and steady steps. Pressing on. This is how to conserve energy. This is how to march steadily through life. Instead of getting too excited, skipping about, or hiking erratically, I try to mimic his style.

The onward march.

Overnight, we slept in long mesh cocoons strung between tall trees at a river's bank. Precisely where panthers come to drink. After night fall, deep in the jungle, a symphony of screams commenced. There is nothing silent about the Amazon at night. The vibrations ricocheted through my body and massaged my being, rocking the hammock. In that moment, I connected to the universe wholeheartedly. We don't need to try to get additional exercise. Being here to experience everything around us is exercise enough. Where trees vibrate and life is a million times more dense than it is possible to comprehend. Life, a million-fold, is all around. Acceptance of everything, it seems, is winning the internal battle.

At sunrise, no one woke me for coffee. The guides and Alejandro let me sleep. Because I'm the Princess. One who needs beauty sleep. And, ideally, coffee, too.

Eventually we set out again. Hiking onward, the local and the Portuguese guides seem to be rationing a small water supply. No one's packing the several litres of H_2O that I so crave in this heat. Nor comforts. Even the beer supply's gone.

Parched. It's worse than hot and balmy. I'm sweating like mad. We keep hiking onward. At this point the soupy liquid inside my rubber boots is tempting to drink. Large blisters are forming on my feet. My body is wet. Then, in sunflecks, immediately dry. That's how fast the dampness evaporates. Instantaneously. The backpack I'm carrying cuts into my skin at the armpits. Despite these conditions, I try not to complain.

I'm the one who asked to be here.

Just when I think I can't continue, my mouth opens but words do not come out. We've arrived at the top of a hill. To my right is a patch of land that used to be jungle. Now ash. The smell of fresh fire laces the air. They call this slash and burn foresting.

Further in front of this clearing are some houses. Wooden boxes on stilts. The roofs serve to collect rainwater. Chickens cluck about under the support beams.

The homeowner approaches us and graciously offers to share whatever we want. I decide not to guzzle this family's water supply because it's probably a sparse commodity. Our guide hands over a long fuzzy cucumber. He produces a knife. Inside the fruit skin, a white fluffy flesh. I can't tell which portion is edible, so I eat the entire thing. Flesh, seed, and rind. Whatever I've eaten, it is moist and sticky and nourishing and satisfying.

Our group advances onward towards more houses. Inside each, I see no furniture, no art, and no electricity. Sitting in each simple box are several children. About ten in each house. The guide is holding a bag of doughnut-like bread. As we pass by, the children approach us. The guide hands me some of the bread. I look at these children and place pastry into tiny outstretched fingers. Just like how some people feed pigeons, I am feeding small children in the Amazon jungle.

The pain of my blisters and chafed skin fades. I am no longer thirsty and annoyed. These smiles are infectious. These smiles are happiness. They make me smile back.

Past the village, a steep bank. In the river below are long boats propelled by a single simple motor at the rear. This river connects to the Amazon River.

This body of water is a vein of life, vaster and more powerful than any vein inside a human body. From the boat, I watch the finger river open gradually, then suddenly onto the Amazon. It is crystal clear in this moment who the victor of my internal battle will be. The realisation of how many people live off this river is a powerful blow. Overwhelming. A gruelling hike to get here was slightly absurd but akin to following a rainbow.

Now for the pot of gold.

November 27, 2010

I ascend to Cielo, or heaven, the fourth story at Andres Carne de Res restaurant in Bogotá. A magnificent meal, dinner theatre, and dance party await to celebrate this adventure and Alejandro, my new boyfriend. A hostess greets our party, taking us to a table. Four low stools set against the dessert kitchen. Above the table is a sign. Orion.

It seems I am following the stars.

7

‖‖‖ ‖‖‖ ‖‖‖ ‖‖‖ ‖‖‖ ‖‖

*"The situations that cause the most frustration
are those that are outside of your control."*

November 29, 2010

It is possible to stop being afraid of your own mind. Living in a foreign country, that some regard as dangerous, with a boyfriend you've just met, might not be the right method for everyone. But it's right for me. This I know because weight is lifting off my shoulders. I feel lighter. There is solace for me to find. The so-called scars in my body can heal.

Released by the weight I'm shedding is a residue of mixed emotions. Ones I know well. Desire, frustration, and anger. A sticky surface that will take time to wipe away. My family, friends, and former colleagues may or may not understand my decision to return home, very briefly, to get rid of all of my things as quickly as possible and return to Colombia.

The Danish man who's sitting beside me in the lounge at El Dorado International Airport seems to find the story compelling. I'm explaining operation dump-it-all to him as we sip on glasses of white wine. In my hand is a pen. On a sheet of paper some words. An attempt to explain things to my mother. I began the note by reminding her how small the world is if we take the time to really sit and talk and listen to one another. I explain the density coming off my back and the clarity replacing it. A vision that tells me it is possible to replace obsessiveness and guilt through education and creativity. That erratic emotional tendencies, sadness, and loneliness will not be large parts of my future self.

I put my pen down because I have too pee. Wandering past a Native American-themed cowboy store towards a washroom, I buy a piece of rhodonite. Not only is it the shape of a heart but also, according to legend, this stone will allow for change. I decide to give this heart-shaped stone to my mother, instead of the letter.

Since I'm not certain how to present Alejandro to anybody that I know back in Canada – how a chocolate bar in a Miami coffee shop led to a few emails led to a three-week-long first date – I'm going to keep details about him to myself. To give up with real estate sales and move in with him, in South America, is precisely what I need right now. This definitely trumps third-party explanation or opinion seeking.

December 7, 2010

My condo is empty. After advertising my former things for free or pocket-change prices on Craigslist, everything vanished rapidly. No more white leather bed frame. No more mirrors. No more couch. No more top-of-the-line printer, fax, and photocopier. No more art. No more stereo. No more dishes. No more plants. All the things I worked so hard to obtain, possessions I took meticulous care and attention in selecting, these things no longer belong to me.

*

December 17, 2010

During a movie, I missed Alejandro's call. He seems absolutely livid. His call is to tell me some rules. Normally, I'm not keen on guidelines. I don't get into this. After getting rid of literally everything I own, my mind is already made up and nothing is going to change it. So I listen up.

Here come the rules.

December 20, 2010

Closing the door on a previous life is to close it on what haunts you. Things like ex-boyfriends, financial irresponsibility, shady real estate clientele, drug addictions, and depression. To have an opportunity for a clean slate and to marvel at life is to have a new sense of possibility.

December 26, 2010

To cope with the overwhelming nature of new surroundings, I cook meals. This is seen as odd amongst my Colombian counterparts because this is what the maid has been hired to do. Oddly, then, I make pasta. Alejandro tells me that it's gourmet. Then, he looks at my hands. At the open sores, scratches, and cuts. He tells my mutilated hands to relax. That I don't need to rush. Not anymore. Not here.

Relax.

This word has echoed in my past. Finally, it's become a word I will start to live by. Saying it internally breaks me down.

December 28, 2010

Alejandro seems to have a good grip on things. In conversation, he reiterates that all it takes to be in a relationship is to know that we're on the same team. Relationships are about give and take. The reward of having someone special at your side outweighs other struggles. I repeat his advice. Over and over.

January 2, 2011

I learn quickly that Alejandro is the boss. We can have a

discussion but his word is final. Rules to abide by include but are not limited to: you must take a shower immediately after going to the gym. You must use the second washroom for the toilet. You must use the en suite off the bedroom for showers.

In addition to Alejandro's rules are his father's. He is the boss of Alejandro. Thankfully, I think relations are amicable. In any hierarchy, liking the king is one thing but remaining in his favour is absolutely critical.

Alejandro tells me that I'm becoming more giving and more willing to compromise and make extra effort to ensure his happiness. It is not clear to me by how much his happiness outweighs my own. Realistically, understanding the complexities of my own happiness right now is difficult. Living abroad in a brand-spanking-new relationship as part of a foreign caste system does that.

The lines are blurred.

January 15, 2011
In front of a fence, a row of white buckets line the sidewalk. Their contents, a cornucopia of roses. Also, my most pressing decision. The bright pink or the even brighter yellow. This is my life. These roses.

When I left Canada I planned to have a financial safety net in terms of savings. I understand that the oceanfront properties I was fired over have indeed sold and that the deal has closed. Despite everything, the seller and his conveyancing lawyer promised me a commission. Unfortunately, it seems that with me taking off abroad, no one has followed through and actually transferred any money.

Absolutely no one is answering any of my queries. All I can see is an empty bank account. It's hard enough to get on the phone, let alone some answers.

To move forward, I try to decide not to take having no money as evidence of failure. I will not continue to fail at everything. At jobs, at relationships, at financial responsibility. This is just going to force me to start again, from scratch. And how good am I at that?

Hiding my despair over this from Alejandro is impossible. However, he finds the scenario comical. According to him, no money and no job is no problem. He tells me not to worry, that I have time.

Covering the house in candy-coloured roses helps only so much. In the thorns, a viral and growing paranoia lives. I'm not sure Alejandro's father likes me as much as I thought he did.

*

January 21, 2011

The gym in Bogotá is a runway showcasing the latest in cosmetic surgery. Here, I allow myself to ogle. Then, include some Yoga after cardio.

Down a steep avenue, I walk to buy candy. Sucking granulated sugar off chewy raspberry, I gaze at the skyline from a park bench near Centro Andino. Most people around here don't believe in walking outside. There are maids for that. Across the playground, someone uniformed walks a dog. In a city of millions, a lack of pedestrians equals privacy.

We are going to a country club tomorrow. I've been introduced to tennis. Striking incoming optic yellow balls with a sturdy racket is an ideal way to deal with frustration. The response must become reflex. Bounce and wait. It seems my natural response to stress, just like my backhand, is to respond too quickly.

All this waiting is hard.

The situations that cause the most frustration are those that are outside of your control. Learning to control your reactions will in turn allow you to change your emotions. Subtle things like muscle tension or tone of voice can influence your thoughts.

This is proven, scientifically.

January 23, 2011

Alejandro's sister has invited me out for drinks. Aside from trips to the beauty salon, it dawns on me that this is the first socialising I have done without my boyfriend. Also, the last.

At a swank patio, slightly separate from others mingling nearby, we sit. The lounge is full, mostly with name-tag-wearing patrons of a petroleum conference being hosted by a well-known financial brokerage. A suited man sends cocktails then comes over to chat. The martinis and introduction lead to a brief discussion on the subject of oil and gas. With my past experience in downstream operations, I waste little time to ask if anyone is hiring. It turns out he is. Mid-beverage, I've been offered a job to work on his growing portfolio of Canadian investors. As in any growth market, the opportunity to make money is alluring.

By the last sip of martini, Alejandro's sister has just one thing to add. She makes herself very clear. Her brother is extremely jealous. Even she doesn't like seeing me talk to another guy. However, she promises not to tell anyone how I found out about the job and encourages me to go for it.

Back at home, forgoing his sister's advice, I tell Alejandro about the employment opportunity. The topic is met with silence. Eventually, he responds. With more rules.

I am not permitted to do anything that will involve long hours or speaking to other men.

January 29, 2011

I made it to the interview on my own. Alejandro did not ask how it went. I suspect he is preoccupied with his own upcoming career move. Specifically, he is set to coordinate and run a private military training camp at one of the family's properties.

Back when it was known as just a vacation property, I visited the estate. It is very rural. Perfect for training armed soldiers. Alejandro made it clear that he wants me to be part of the project. To do what, I have no idea. As if sensing my sentiment, his father has suggested that I offer the men Yoga classes.

For someone who feels slightly useless at the moment, teaching Yoga to soldiers at a military camp is utility. Just not exactly what I had in mind.

January 31, 2011
Alejandro's father is saying something to him about my wardrobe. In Spanish. Something about it being too flashy. Alejandro neglects to translate the message. He does this routinely. More reason for the Spanish text book I've been studying. Third-party translation becomes less and less necessary.

*

February 2, 2011
I've become all natural in this setting. There are no beauty treatments or shops. We're off the grid too. There's no Internet, smart phones, computers, or even air conditioning.

I don't have lots of experience with wellness retreats. I imagine part of the allure is designating a period of time to get away. Then one goes back to their normal routine. To feel good without modern convenience helps you to feel good on other levels. From our current coordinates, just south of the equator at a farm that's far away from even a tiny village, I have time to think about living in isolation. My difficulty is the realisation that I have no normal routine to go back to.

On the agenda in the meantime, absolutely nothing. If I want, I'm allowed to offer Yoga to the soldiers. My previous pastime, cooking, is irrelevant. There are some groceries but, in this extreme heat, eating is seldom. There are also the maids.

The thermometer on the post of the gondola reads thirty-eight degrees Celsius, in the shade. I sit adjacent to a turquoise pool. The white plastic furniture is supernaturally white. Sushi and Sashimi are nearby. My home comforts. It turns out that they enjoy the heat. Alejandro is in the distance with thirty-four other men. The soldiers in training.

Before we left Bogotá, by searching Wikipedia, I read a few articles about private security and on mercenary. Given that I have zero familiarity with anything to do with local or international military, I felt the need for a minor education. What I now understand is that for a private military person to be a candidate for a professional contract, he or she must pass a standard physical test. This involves running a certain distance in a certain amount of time, and executing a certain number of push-ups and sits-ups in a certain amount of time. The operation I am witnessing is like a CrossFit gym for Colombian men who have been recruited here. These men already have a local military background because that's mandatory in this country. Hence the soldiers we saw in the Amazon. It turns out that one can go onto a career afterwards in private international military. I don't suppose, whether someone is hired locally or abroad to a conflict zone, that they will be paid much. This is the international economic appeal of these men. They're relatively cheap.

February 3, 2011

Daylight is intensified this close to the equator. It's like colour-land. Bright hand-woven red and purple striped fabric cradles me in the hammock in which I sway. At night-time, my body still rocks.

At the main house, I have hooked up music to the soldier's auditory system. This area, designated to show videos on safety formations, knife fights, car bombs, and violent movies, is also perfect as a private Yoga *sala*. To complement my practice, I explore Zen meditation. Sitting and doing nothing at all. At a private military camp, while thirty-four men learn better form in which to kill in the name of protection, I find Zen.

Sipping white wine from an aluminum tumbler while sitting under my favourite constellation, Orion, is bliss. The black-ink sky illuminates the lime and mango trees. They become like cartoons. The radio plays salsa and merengue love songs. Insects in the distance dance and sing along. I can smell flowers. Rose and gardenia. The hacienda and the entire property are all quiet. The men are off for a long run. I've also been out running. Not with the men but on my own. Alejandro won't let me go off the property alone so keeps surveillance by driving just behind me.

At his discretion I either turn around or get in the car and we return to the camp. Otherwise, with him watching over my back, I've been running. In the forty-degree heat, I run. The path is along a black tar road where a construction crew paves the way. The sun reflects against fresh asphalt, tanning my skin to a dark copper. Sweat pours out of every pore on my body. My breathing becomes slow, relaxed, and steady. Each breath cools me.

My breath is permanently slowed. This morning I ran a little farther, scanning the farms in the horizon and the dirt road that continues far beyond where I run or where my eyes can see. This distance tempts me. The road ahead is the only temptation at military camp. Otherwise, no one looks at me and no one dares talk to me. This is isolation.

In silence. And invisible.

6

‖‖‖ ‖‖‖ ‖‖‖ ‖‖‖ ‖‖‖ ‖‖

"The nooks and crannies of the psyche live in the body."

February 4, 2011

The dogs play between the gondola's shade and the lawn. Their handmade ribbon dog leashes shine brilliant in the sunlight. Bright pink and lime green. Like ribbons streaming from a maypole. In my hands, a strong coffee. The sweetness of condensed milk is indulgence.

Not written on the pages of the Spanish text book that I'm reading is how much I like it here. Not because I actually like it here. But because I like myself.

February 5, 2011

Instead of the men dining off-property, the maid started cooking for the camp. Even in rural Colombia it's not wise to draw overt attention to this operation. I'm not eating whatever they eat. I'm not eating much at all. Instead, I munch on a terribly bitter spiny sprig of the *savilla* plant. My entire body is covered in this cool, clear fluid. The gel is in my hair and in my mouth. I'm going to nap covered in aloe in the hammock while the electric fan circles above, humming.

When I wake, from far away, the men grunt as they count push-ups or shoot muffled guns at a target. They yell words of instruction and encouragement. These men follow a strict routine. Bed time. Meal times. Training times. I follow no schedule beyond the rising and setting of the sun. Because of this, even though I can hear them, at the same time, I hear absolutely nothing at all.

Solitude is really cool. For a while. Then the wish to have someone to drink chilled white wine and share jokes with invades the wide open spaces. Alejandro's idea of sharing is to ignore me. He prefers to spend all of his time with the soldiers. An authentic military experience. Suitable because he's training rigorously. Not because he has to, but for his own pleasure.

February 6, 2011

Some things we go through are too painful to remember. Things we cry over until our eyes, red and raw, run out of tears. The hardest emotional breakdowns we try to block from memory. To uncover what's been buried, we can look to our muscles, joints, and tendons. The nooks and crannies of the psyche live in the body. Here, the past looks surreal. Like it belongs to a movie that we vaguely remember seeing.

In intense heat and intense Yoga *asanas*, I recover some of what is hidden in my body. Sitting cross-legged on my mat and eating dripping red watermelon, my belly is full. There's plenty more fresh watermelon. Plus, an abundance of the here and now.

In the river, cool water flows over Alejandro's body and over mine. Anchored to a rock, I still don't know if what I think is shared aloud. The river flooded over the winter, changing the landscape and depositing sand and pieces of tree everywhere. We blend in with the flood debris.

It's dawning on me that maybe I don't need a job, or Alejandro, or anything else.

February 7, 2011

I'm told that things are going well and that we will be spending more time at the military camp. Since this is not my property and not my business, I do not respond. I don't tell Alejandro that if his family continues to use the property as a full-time military operation it will lose its charm. I don't tell him that I do not wish to live much longer at an isolation retreat. I don't say anything.

Smiling and nodding, I peer along the river into the distance. Past a bridge, towards a triangular-shaped mountain.

February 8, 2011

I'm crying. It's been hard to stop but necessary to hide. Alejandro doesn't want to see me cry. At night, our dreams hold clues. Mine tell me to communicate with someone away from here.

From beside his hand gun, I take Alejandro's Blackberry and download my email account. The first message in the inbox is about the work venture that I've been unable to formally accept. They would like to send me to attend a tradeshow in the United States. I envision possibilities. Including the mall beside the convention centre and English-speaking, civilian company. The only barrier, Alejandro's vocalisation that I am not allowed to work long hours, or around other men.

I decide to try to convince him of the suitability of the opportunity. I am met with silence so leave to follow it to the only place I'm allowed to go to alone. The river.

Walking upstream, the round river rocks turn to soft white sand. Beach-like and pink-hued. I'm crying once more. At this point I want a break from doing self-improvement. To stop the tears, I just accept that I have a way to go to get to whatever happens next.

While I wade along the riverbank, it starts to rain. The shower intensifies and I am quickly soaking wet. Drinking it in. A storm rolls in. Everything intensifies. It's loud, magnificent, slightly terrifying, and utterly romantic.

February 9, 2011

Sneaking onto Alejandro's phone again, I share my passport information and confirm attendance at the forbidden tradeshow.

I then try to go about the rest of the day casually.

The screaming of nocturnal insects wakes me. Sunset here is 6 pm. At sundown, it's the insects who cry.

*

February 10, 2011

There is a slightly cross-eyed man who wears wool socks that peek out from his thick leather work boots. His green cargo pants are tucked into these socks. A flannel shirt (over a white crew neck) is tucked into his waistband, cinched tightly way above his waistline with a military belt. He's called Manuel. He's always running around and standing at attention when other people, like Alejandro, speak to him. His current job is to retrieve an errant ball from the grass and return it to the water polo game the soldiers are playing in the swimming pool. Alejandro, the referee, sits at the side of the pool, in the centre. On his head, the kind of hat with a brim all the way around, beige cotton, and washed hundreds of times. The hat's chord, snug under his chin. This type of hat irritates me. However, it's the reason why Alejandro's face isn't covered in weird stains, freckles, and other sun spots. I look down to my hands.

When they're done, the men line up before Alejandro for him to pour rubbing alcohol directly into their ears. This kills any parasites that may have gotten into the ear canal.

February 11, 2011

Hand freckles intensifying, Alejandro's theory is lime juice as the culprit. Apparently, real Colombian women know better than to go near limes. Apparently, they won't even take a garnished cocktail. I am evidence that haphazard zesting leads to haphazard freckling.

Out of the corner of my eye, something fluorescent flies out from the tree and across the pool. Unreal orange and green and blue plumage. Like a pack of colouring pens, a giant parrot.

It's time to mark the road for the soldier's timed run. Alejandro anticipates an eleven-minute mile. I tell him how impressively fast this is. Flattery, that's met with standstill. Alejandro approaches me with his cell phone. It's a call about the tradeshow. I don't know what to do. Alejandro is demanding that I log into my email account and let him read everything. Aside from feeling furious that there's a concealed Internet connection, I wince.

He reads some emails and seems conflicted. Part of him understands my independence. Another part refuses it. Instead of being disagreeable, I call his sister for the opposite of a reassuring conversation. Her English is good enough to express that, no matter what I get into, I will be seen as scandalous by her family. Again, her brother is jealous. I'm his property and no one, not even their father, is going to intervene to give any advice on the situation.

She leaves me with some final advice. To cut my losses and get out while I still can.

The birds begin to chirp in unison. They're loud. My mood is rapidly changing. I don't feel alarmed but rather disgusting and worthless. I need a cold shower and to order a pizza. Luxuries that don't exist in these outcroppings.

February 12, 2011

I decide that life is too short to sit around and worry. Instead, listening to Mozart, I sip piping-hot coffee and marvel over how the blue sky contrasts perfectly against the green tree canopy. My shadow looks at me. In it I see three tiers of ruffled sleeves on a cotton heather grey dress. I've dressed like the birds. Winged. Ready to fly away.

But first, I convince myself that Alejandro isn't my enemy. Making plans without consulting him was selfish.

I stop and begin to listen.

To the music and the birds.

To everything.

*

February 13, 2011

The word of the day. *Jugar*. A game.

Life is a game. It really is.

People who see playing as childish, don't prosper. The most successful and happy adults, still play. Beside me is a burning fire and beyond it, the men shoot at targets. Their muffled barrels crackle just like the flames.

February 14, 2011

I brought up the topic of leaving the camp, innocently, at the lunch table. Alejandro's response, to flip it on me. Not the subject but the entire table.

Embarrassed, I stormed away. In hot pursuit, he followed behind me. Back at our private quarters, he got on the phone to instruct the maid back home, in English, to take my things and dump them onto the street. A scenario I am not agreeable to. To protest, I grabbed the phone. He reacted instantaneously, to grab my arm and leverage me forward to smash my head into the floor.

Holding me by the hair he slams my head a few more times, for good measure, then presses my face firmly against the floor. Bone crushing tile. Tile crushing bone.

Everything.

Stops.

The silver pistol, inches away from our confrontation, smells like metal. The words coming out of Alejandro's mouth register with me in slow motion.

If I make a scene, I am dead. If I think that there is anyone who's going to stop him from dragging me by the hair down to the river to drown me right now, then I should think again.

No one will blink an eye.

Interestingly, I'm not thinking about the value of my life. It's very clear, currently, that it doesn't hold much. I'm thinking about my hair. The bits of it missing from my scalp.

If our roles were reversed and I was ripping out Alejandro's expensive hair-transplant-surgery hair, the words coming from his mouth would not be threats. If I ever pulled his hair, he would, in fact, kill me.

I decide hair will grow back, life isn't fair, and play dead.

5

𝍷𝍷𝍷𝍷 𝍷𝍷𝍷𝍷 𝍷𝍷𝍷𝍷 𝍷𝍷𝍷𝍷 𝍷𝍷𝍷𝍷 𝍷𝍷

"I am trying to act very neutral but inside I am very sad."

February 15, 2011

I am entirely ready to conclude this retreat. This experiment. Whatever it has been. I would like it to be over now.

After the altercation, on his order, I follow Alejandro to the river. The same one I've been luxuriating in. The same one he threatened to drown me in.

I stand at the bank and watch him get into the water, sit down, and physically cool off. He invites me to get in as well. Of course I do not want to be anywhere near him or the goddamn river. Still standing at the bank, trembling, I shake my head. No. This, the only thing I am sure of.

I will not get into the water.

His words are slow. They say, he's letting me go. I accept this and wonder if I have time to pack. This is a trip I wish I looked slightly better for. Any combination of a shower, some make-up, an ID, and money would go a long way. Accepting everything is to continue to stand. In slow motion, the surroundings appear larger than in real life. Everything is magnified.

Alejandro planned to drop me off at a bus stop. But he didn't buy a ticket and didn't drive me there either.

I am trying to act very neutral but inside I am very sad.

To get beaten and hear words about how swiftly your life can be taken away is sad. The fact that no one intervened is sad.

These things are all overwhelmingly sad.

I close my eyes and envision a light installation, illuminated thousands of kilometres away atop the Keefer Hotel in East Vancouver.

Everything is going to be alright.

*

February 16, 2011

I finally left the military camp.

From inside this hotel, I could be anywhere in the world. With standardized settings, like a queen bed flanked by two side tables, over-priced bottled water, a small office, and a television, there's no distinction.

We didn't come straight to this hotel. Instead, Alejandro took me first to the ranch.

When we got there, I sat on the Persian rug in front of the stone mantelpiece and enormous fireplace. The maid had built a fire. Looking at the flames, I thought back to four months ago at this precise location. Where I decided to get over my fear of the unknown and unconditionally trust the world. In front of the fire this time, I begged Alejandro to relax. Finally I got to give, not receive, this word. He didn't listen though. I told him I came to Colombia to make Peace. Not War.

His response, to laugh at me. Then, drink an entire bottle of tequila. Then, thoroughly beat me.

This is what it feels like to open my eyes from a four-month blink.

Open, my eyes hurt because they're swollen. Burgeoning salty tears burn whatever swollen skin and exposed flesh they roll down. Pain that over the course of the day has become more mental than physical. A significant transition.

Covered in bruises, I emerged from the ranch bed this morning, nearly tripping on a carton of Aguardiente. Gulping it had been medicinal at one point. But the hangover came quick. I needed a toilet and to throw up. Passing the double mirrored closet doors, I spied my naked body. The entirely of it covered in marks and red welts. Belt lashings. My flesh, resembling a bruised banana.

In unscathed form, lying on the bed back in the room, Alejandro was silent.

As a piece of decaying fruit, I would like to laugh at myself. To test whether laughter can help me to forget. Whether it can transform the sharp sting of being hit by his open hand or aid in the ability to forget what it's like to relax when someone is abusing you.

Sometimes it's OK to laugh at yourself. This morning, for example, I needed to.

But it's nine hours later now and there's nothing left to laugh about.

Alejandro stopped by the clubhouse to take in the end of a mid-morning polo match. I stood back on the patio. Bewildered. Someone else there to watch, asked, incredulous, what are you doing here?

Then we drove onward to Bogotá and Alejandro pulled into a restaurant. This, his idea of being nice. Taking the battered ex-girlfriend out in public to dine beside a child's birthday party. Even though I looked like someone who had just been violently raped, I ordered the pasta primavera. He, a personal-size pizza with pesto and capicola ham.

It would have be nice to savour for the last time the resident freshly-squeezed orange juice, but after physical abuse even the most succulent citrus has no flavour.

Food just fills the pit in your stomach.

It dawned on me just how ugly I felt when Alejandro opened his mouth, in a whisper, to announce that it was time to go.

His father and maid had packed my things. It was all waiting at a hotel nearby.

Before I could respond, he warned me not to make a scene. As if I had the energy for that. I barely had enough energy to walk out.

He grabbed my arm to lead me away. I looked back at the restaurant and regretted not ordering food for the road. The journey back from this particular break-up will be long. I might get hungry.

At the hotel, I feel too large for the room. Alejandro has the nerve to state how nice the place is. All I see is bad interior decoration and poor lighting. There aren't any fresh flowers or a mini bar. I say nothing, continuing to cry instead.

Somehow I had become detached from everything that's been going on and it's like my nerves are only just reconnecting to my brain. As a whole, everything is crying in pain. The blackness of this pain is impossible to conceal.

Two large luggage trollies arrive to the room. They carry seven large cardboard boxes and six suitcases. Crushed, dirty boxes and ripped, gnarly suitcases with wires that protrude from the corners. Despite how battered this luggage appears, each box is carefully labelled with a handwritten description of its contents.

Alejandro then asks if I would like to come back home with him. Says he's unsure about the break-up.

Mustering all that remains as rational energy, I tell him that I need to rest. Alone.

Times like these are impervious to clock time.

Alejandro instructs his chauffeur to wait out front. Tomorrow he will move my things back into the property they've just been moved out of. Then, we hug. An honest hug. He doesn't know it, but this is goodbye. And it really hurts.

The door clicks shuts and I slide the chain lock into place. An auto-pilot mode kicks in. I fill an ash tray with kibble and another with water to accommodate the dogs. Then, I go to the washroom mirror. My reflection doesn't offer any clues.

I imagine myself filling the bath tub. I imagine myself half-submerged, the water continuing to fill the porcelain casket. Wet clothes simultaneously cling to the body and float up around the neck and face. A warm layer of water bubbles between skin and cloth. With one leg extended up the wall and the other bent over the side of the tub, I imagine keeping my head underwater.

Wanting to die.

I stop imagining things and comb my hair, wash, and apply lotion.

February 17, 2011

I dial a country code, long distance number, and ten digits. A numerical sequence etched in my memory.

Denton picks up the phone. The words exchanged are in slight panic. Every sentence is a tiny fight. Technically, I have an outgoing flight from Colombia to the United States booked on the ancient pretense that I would attend an oil and gas tradeshow. I can make the flight if I get in a taxi within ten minutes. I am asking him if this is a suitable escape plan. I seem to think it is.

Unfortunately, my passport is missing.

Denton's advice is to forget the airport, to forget my things, and to leave the hotel for another location. Immediately. This is contrary to what I had in mind. I want to go to Alejandro's condo and confront him about the passport. I end the conversation and quickly consolidate various boxed contents down to an emergency suitcase and leave the hotel.

Without hesitation or scrutiny for Alejandro's chauffeur parked nearby, I enter a black town car. The driving instructions seem surreal. To the Canadian Embassy. *Por favor.*

*

February 20, 2011

Like most secure government buildings, entering with animals is problematic. Waiting with them in the lobby, a woman named Manuella has arrived. She is the cousin of a half-Colombian cross-dressed man I met one time at a Halloween party. She is here to help me out even though I am a perfect stranger.

With Manuella, Colombia is very nice. We shop, dine, dance, attend an art gallery, and chat. All pleasantries that distract from my reality. After dark, I'm tormented by indescribable nightmares.

From severely restless sleep, I wake up not knowing where I am.

According to the postal address on the complimentary pad of paper on the nightstand, I'm at the Radisson hotel located across from the Canadian Embassy in Bogotá. Travis and DP arranged this accommodation to cover me while an emergency passport is issued. Logistically, this will require paperwork, documents, photographs, flight details, police reports, and translated statements.

The emergency passport process will take five days. An official promised me this. Wavering, I go to the spa. This seems a smart move. Gingerly, the technician caresses my aching body and says nothing about the cuts and bruises. To finish, she looks deep into my eyes and tells me that I am beautiful.

I wish I could believe her.

A week ago I may have done. Today it's much more difficult. Oh these lingering ugly feelings.

February 26, 2011

With an exit visa and temporary passport, I return to Canada. Not that I know exactly where to go. But I need a friend.

The reception is cold. Not just in temperature. I arrive to an interrogation at customs and a message from Barby. Who I thought might take me in. Through the medium of voicemail, she talks of how she feels bad about what happened. But that she doesn't want to hang out with a rumoured escort. As in the variety men pay to spend time with. This could mar her reputation.

Upon hearing audible hysterics, the border patrol agent eases off his questioning. These tears taste so stale by this point. I'm going to stop crying.

With little choice, Travis lets me come over. I'm interrupting his romantic Valentine's weekend. So I hide out in the guest room. Specifically, the walk-in closet. In here it's dark and silent.

It turns out that my experiment of life therapy is what others, frankly, describe as recklessness.

From the floor of the walk-in closet at Travis's, I decide to leave for a place where acceptance is guaranteed.

4

HHl HHl HHl HHl HHl ll

"The relationship you have with food is directly related
to the comfort you have in your own skin."

February 28, 2011

The last time I was at my grandparent's in Montreal, I was
sixteen. Somehow over a decade has passed since then. To
return to any place you haven't seen in a while is worthwhile. In
my case, to live here has been on a list of personal goals that was
written several years ago and since forgotten.

It turns out that the order of reaching a goal doesn't matter.
You simply must continue to strive. It turns out that it is possible
to get everything you want. Just not necessarily in the order you
had in mind.

Rediscovering these forgotten goals, and encountering the
special affection of grandparents, I feel aware. That my system's
still in shock.

March 20, 2011

I am rather upset with Barby for questioning what kind of
person I am. As if I didn't thoroughly try to have a normal
romantic life? I feel robbed of the material possessions I've
recently abandoned. And still hurt from the violent nature in
which I left Colombia.

My dreams are laced with regret over not getting revenge. But
there is a silver lining. Each morning my grandmother sings out
bonjour and asks how I slept. Over tea with honey, I will recover.

I decide to tour Montreal's Yoga studios and enjoy Grandma's loving, nourishing, and inspiring company. With a best friend like her, a new kind of time emerges. A clock that chimes in French. My homework is this language. It's a step towards remembering a language long forgotten.

Self-understanding.

For once I am not sinking into full-on depression.

On the contrary, the simple things in life taste, look, and feel better than ever. Even though my trust and self-esteem appear ruined, they are actually growing strong.

March 21, 2011

It is necessary to maintain that I shouldn't apologise and I don't have anything to be sorry for. There is nothing wrong with being an adventuress. There is nothing wrong with a brief and passionate relationship with a South American Polo Ralph Lauren model lookalike. With all the lying, scamming, two-timing, and exploiting that goes on in this world, people need to stop apologising outwardly for that which doesn't warrant it. Instead of resentment, be reminded not to participate in hateful petty gossip or malicious treatment of others. In time, you can forget the desire to condemn.

I have to remind myself daily that we travel to gain what can't be bought. The real riches. Life. Not falling into my old bad habits, that is the ongoing work.

March 30, 2011

My digestion and intestinal function are awry. I crave thousands of calories but cannot go more than twenty-four hours without throwing up. This isn't an instance of making myself puke with an oblong object. Impressive stomach spasms and acid reflux do it automatically now. What category of bulimia is that?

Quickly bloated and overweight, jeans suffocate the excess floatation device that's formed around my waist. They cut inward and reveal a loathsome muffin-top. Thank God for stretch pants. At least weight gain also goes to the boobs. No one detests ample cleavage.

Food, as a Band-Aid to violence we've submitted our body to, can become food to nourish and support an unscathed body. The relationship you have with food is directly related to the comfort you have in your own skin.

Conclusion: I am uncomfortable.

Yoga explains emotional eating through blockage or unbalance in the energy centres. These chakras are supposed to exist in unison with the universe. They turn as wheels of life. Located near the throat is the centre that governs metabolism and the ability to express yourself. In the navel, your intuition and digestion. Emotions live near the heart's centre. Maelstrom of any kind can throw these energy centres off kilter. They can become unbalanced. Symptomatically, my body's ability to speak, trust, digest, and feel is amuck. I'm blocked, but aware of it. That counts for something.

All things to ponder over another serving of Grandma's quiche.

*

April 1, 2011

I can't seem to help myself from being asked out. My first date is with a local tax lawyer. Him and I just did everything that's amazing to do at a Porsche dealership. This was before the date ended in a conniption. Not because he wants to trade in for another model. For successful men who drive luxury import vehicles, the ability to trade in for a newer model always exists. This doesn't bother me. It was when he told me to fuck off that

I took offence. Something about his time being coveted and me not actually wanting to date anyone.

I'm OK with banter, going for meals, and shopping. If I get drunk I could even be OK to fool around. Though this would contradict my asexuality pact. An agreement designed to keep my vulnerability protected. However, I am presently sober so it follows that an invitation to his secluded woodland cottage is outside of my comfort zone. And impossible. So I declined. And he objected.

I held my mouth shut and looked straight ahead past everything. At the periphery, calmly requesting to be dropped off.

April 4, 2011

I begin to attend the local church. With my grandma. Here the light shines inwards through stained glass installations. These rays reflect onto a statue of Jesus.

Que la paix soit avec vous.

Sitting in pews, we turn to shake hands with our neighbours. Peace. As someone formerly at war, these words no longer elicit emotion beyond sitting here. It's warming. The Spring of Peace.

*

April 8, 2011

This is how things unravel. I burnt my face with a do-it-yourself 40% glycolic acid peel and am at a hotel. With another guy. Turns out I'm on another date.

The gymnasium has space to practise Yoga. I try to centre myself.

Afterwards, I spot a brown paper bag. Inside is what looks to be a healthy snack. The label says BK Buddha. Apparently it's organic and gluten free. Fancy. For a pot cookie.

Edible THC leaves me unravelling like a kite string. I fly around in sequined shorts and a velvet bow tie that my date has purchased for me as a gift. Dressed in new clothing for the night, I gravitate towards salted peanuts being served alongside drinks at the lobby bar. I've just gone swiftly back to being someone who likes to party with random company. Getting stoned. And munching. I don't even remember the guy's name. I simply file him in my phone as 'Date Apr 8' in case I later need something I think he can provide.

Afterwards I've lost my voice and have what feels like bronchitis of the lungs.

April 10, 2011

It has not taken much time for me to end up at one of Montreal's infamous strip clubs.

I ignore the gorgeous women and other patrons and prowl around the upper level private dance corridor for a vending machine that sells snacks. I find one near the back. Unfortunately, it doesn't function. The management seems entertained by my request to come fix the problem.

On an energy level, eating food all the time has a grounding effect. A direction that can quell other temptations. The more I keep eating, the less I crave anything else.

But what to do with my mind? It's having some quite serious episodes. One happened on the way home, in the back of a taxi. It is entirely possible that the driver was taking me home, as asked. Suddenly, though, the space between the rear bench and passenger seat had shrunk. There was no longer room for my legs. Exactly like being in the back of a police car. I started to panic. Was I in a taxi or, possibly, had I been arrested?

My imagined scenario felt so real. A panic attack? A psychotic episode? It's some kind of lapse in reality. Thankfully, I've made it home and sought my grandma.

239

April 11, 2011

Grandma is upstairs preparing coffee. She thinks I was drugged last night. I was honest with her, that sometimes I have been eating treats that contain THC.

Without judgement, Grandma thinks this is a good thing to happen, a lesson not to consume strange things.

You have to be careful, she tells me.

*

April 15, 2011

I don't waste any more time to find a job. It's in a hotel lounge.

April 30, 2011

I mostly do not feel very pretty. My skin has recovered. So onto it I apply make-up. Being chatty and pleasant to customers is quite easy. But I have to gear up to this type of acting. This was all going fine up until my level of French speaking became an issue. One of the customers complained about me.

I've learned that in Montreal there is a language police. Their job is to ensure the strength of the language. It is illegal to work until one speaks fluently. So I've been dismissed. Luckily one of my colleagues has recommended something else, a replacement job. Where I will be bartending now and then at anglophone weddings.

May 3, 2011

It's safe to say that, even though my employment status is rickety, Montreal is a Game Changer. This expression, my current Mantra. Changing the game is a precursor to taking things to the next level. The former refers to anything that has the power to improve a situation. The latter holds the unlimited possibility of what's next.

The things we usually need to change range from the subtle, like the type of music we listen to, to the substantial, like forgoing alcoholism and bulimia. The game is that change is not necessarily immediate. Instant gratification usually comes from things that are not sustainable. So, to truly change, we must identify the end of a cycle and reduce the amount of time resting in the interim. Staying too long in the wrong place or mindset, you risk to give up.

Trust, like change, also doesn't happen overnight. Especially if you've ever been traumatized. These days, I attempt to face the truth by holding no one but myself accountable.

Accountability prevents an array of false expectations. Expectations in general, I have learned, are a sure way to disappointment. Expectations are not reality.

May 8, 2011

The post-Colombia nightmares stopped because I buried them in my grandma's garden. No longer do I wake up not knowing where I am. For the most part, I'm at my grandparents'.

Bartending hadn't lured me into full-time excessive drinking.

But then my friend Lana came to play and I met someone else while out dancing with her. And he likes to heavy pour.

We met originally underneath the city, standing in a candle-lit and stone-fortified corridor. He paid for our coat check. Before mentioning that he recently wrote a novel, he casually mentioned how he's Scandinavian. That or his chewing tobacco is. Neither fact matters because, of determinate origin, shots of tequila arrived.

A tequila night can easily evaporate away to a humid day. My transportation right now is a vintage 1970's 8 speed bike, a gift from Grandma's neighbour. And all I want to pedal towards is this man who is going to enable me. Christian. He is inside a townhouse with a friend and they are drinking a combination of wine and vodka. It's noon, or, their happy hour.

After re-introducing myself as the woman from the coat check last night, I am intrigued as well by the friend. He's handsome and disconnected. He looks precisely like how I feel.

I show them some Yoga by pressing into a full handstand against the brick wall. I hope that going upside down underneath the skylight will realign my chakras. I hope that if I can still do this it will mean that I am sober. However, just because I can do a handstand doesn't mean a thing. The three of us are absolutely wasted.

Christian's lips are rimmed with red wine. His eyes are all over the place but straighten momentarily to look deeply into mine. He instructs me to go home, change, and come back out with them.

Upon my return, donning red, Christian clearly hasn't stopped drinking. Even though he cannot open his eyes at this point, he tells me I look better. A tiny compliment I am so desperate to hear. To take him out, me and his friend have to support his entire body weight.

When Christian nearly fell out the door of a moving taxi we decided to return to the house. Back around the kitchen table, there is more wine and I attempt to converse about balance. I tell them about a motivational podcast I listened to the other day. Christian's opinion on such a podcast, loosely translated from Russian by his friend, is "Eat shit you cunt." His final words before passing out face-first on the table.

I am attracted to the probability of being deeply hurt by a man like Christian. A nasty alcoholic. This is because I am still masochistic.

May 9, 2011

At sunrise, Christian, his friend, and I go for breakfast somewhere with white tablecloths and a bay window overlooking the cobbled streets of St. Paul *Ouest*. A slightly overcast sky gives a matte quality to the silverware. A baked brie arrives. For some reason I know that if I eat the entire thing I will be met with ridicule, so I just have a little.

For some reason I feel sober right now. Likely, desensitization.

Christian explains to me how most people are extremely buttoned up. A state of being, he says, that we're not in. I understand that, most often, responsibility seems boring but also that I am in the midst of serious bender. I leave him again. This time with the mindset to go and sew buttons onto several shirts.

But first, I have a few flights to catch.

3

||||| ||||| ||||| ||||| ||||| ||

*"The shame itself of what I've been reduced to
feels like a miscarriage of my soul."*

May 14, 2011

Barby is going to have a hen do in Las Vegas. I'm not sure exactly where my relationship with her stands, but I have been invited to this event. To be one of her girlfriends and wear matching bikinis at her party.

My original excuse was not having enough money to attend. What I meant by money was self-confidence. Barby, like anyone busy planning a wedding, doesn't know how vulnerable I am these days. So, like a good friend would, she's put in a request to a Venezuelan man, a mutual acquaintance of ours from Miami, to fly me out to Vegas.

I met the Venezuelan after emerging from his shower. Back then, I slathered on golden sparkly lotion and he handed me a fluorescent T-shirt to wear as a dress. The slogan 'I'm in Miami Bitch' seemed a perfect sentiment for a ride in his red Ferrari. We went out for an hour's worth of high-end shopping. Thousand-dollar red-soled shoes and designer purses don't buy themselves, do they? They can be purchased through financial sponsorship. The kind of thing South Beach revolves around.

That all seems a million years ago now. Presently, I'm not sure I'm able to be the person that this man and Barby expect. I've been through too much since then and can't seem to get myself in the right mood on demand.

May 22, 2011

Without qualm, I seem to have no problem travelling with Sam though. At the cost of over eleven grand for three days with him in Barbados, you'd think it'd make me feel amazing. Judging by how it contained straight vodka for the 6 am outbound flight, my water bottle is evidence for why I feel like shit.

Despite this, in Barbados I hired a tennis instructor. I went to the gym. I tried to practise my Yoga. On the pavilion this afternoon, beachside, with a mat between sand and Sandy Lane, and a tree canopying the movements. Gesturing to the waves as they break and retreat, I stretch. My muscles manage to relax. I sink deeper.

Wide-eyed, a boy comes to face me and begins to mimic the *asanas*. As he copies me I can imagine what it's like to teach Yoga and I like it. To be a teacher do I have to be pure and unwounded? To teach do I have to forget about the temporary passport that I'm travelling on or my seeming inability to achieve moderation?

The energy around myself and this boy softens. My heartbeat slows down as I share Yoga with some kid who has no idea what Yoga even is. There is hope. I would like to be a Yoga teacher one day.

*

May 24, 2011

Interestingly, I found the passport thought to be stolen by Alejandro. It turned up safely among items in a file marked 'Personal'. Holding it in my hands allows me to forgive him. Turns out, I am extremely good at forgiving other people.

May 31, 2011

I have continued to see Christian. Continued to drink way too much. I have lost my cell phone. And my Gucci hat. But I have managed to arrive in Las Vegas for Barby's hen. A shuttle drops me off from the airport to the Cosmopolitan, a dark hotel where the Venezuelan is staying. My plan is to say thank you. And hang out a little. But he hasn't checked in. All I have is ninety dollars. Cash stuffed in my pocket. And some time to kill.

The lobby lounge gleams, shiny with chandeliers made of black lacquer. A gin and soda will do in this setting. With a drink in hand, bar side, I pivot left towards two guys who sit beside me. This is how to meet people. Via slight pivot.

The one closest is called Cole. He'd be the bad-boy slash paragon cast in a British gangster movie. Ex-construction worker turned businessman. With a witty personality and all the muscles. A gin and soda later, Cole and I are together. A good way to get to know someone. His kisses are delicious and I like it. He jokes about a shot-gun wedding, Vegas-style. How fun. Someone who likes the same little game that I do. I say let's do it. His allure is powerful and I immediately forget about Barby, her party, and the Venezuelan. By the time our subsequent rounds of gin are finished we learn that it is too late to get a marriage permit so we leave instead to Cole's hotel room to consummate all the things left unsaid.

His room has a great view. Great room service. And the boutique convenience store beside the lobby elevator is selling all the right kinds of creams and products to help with beautification. It's almost like going to the spa, except I'm going to be doing the work myself. I came here feeling quite dispirited. But in this setting, with Cole, I manage to blossom.

June 1, 2011

I wake before him and do my nails. The nail polish is light purple. Lavender. I unpack lingerie to wear for breakfast. It is black and white and red. *Très* French maid. I play music as the sun rises over Las Vegas Boulevard. The concrete jungle, sleeping at dawn, is awakening.

Cole and his friend want to drive to California, and I want to accompany them. After all, to be at the ocean is to feel even better. It's called the City of Angels and the one flying over me has a real sense of humour.

She didn't issue a warning about bath salts.

*

June 2, 2011

My Californian weekend with Cole is going well. We're hanging out like two people who have known one another for a considerable time. It's comfortable. Until we hit the LA nightclub scene. Getting in, cocktails and dancing weren't a problem. It was the final stop of the evening: a convenience store in Hollywood. Somewhere to buy legitimate items: menthol cigarettes (for the guys), gum, water, and red licorice (for me). It's here where things went awry. The bath salts were on display inconspicuously on the countertop beside the till. The back of the package reads 'Not for Human Consumption', but they're here for sale, to inhale, anyway. I don't have a little voice inside telling me not to buy such a thing. Not to try it.

Back at the hotel, one, admittedly large, line later, and I am on a rocket to total nervous overstimulation. They call this legal highs. But for me it's an all-time low. This random concoction. Whatever it actually is. Mixed with alcohol and an empty stomach. Has delivered an outcome of mental overload, but a body disconnected from her control centre. It just shakes.

Despite this debilitation, I go to bed with Cole.

Lights low. Camera. Action.

We become disfigured bodies contorting to rub together genitals. To achieve or deliver pleasure is instinctual, after all. It doesn't require higher brain activity or functional fine and gross motor skills. It's like a mating male mantis who keeps thrusting toward semen delivery even after his female counterpart has devoured his head.

Because I can't really move I'm lying on my back and Cole is on top of me, facing away. Reverse cowgirl. Except he's the rider. I have inserted a formerly empty 26 oz bottle of vodka into his anus. It's now siphoning brownish fluid which streams downwards. Soiling both the bed and myself.

This must stop. Please.

As Cole sinks into a deep sleep, I crawl down from the bed to the floor. As the jitters intensify, some sort of paralysis ensues. My body will not respond to any direction my mind is giving it. I begin to sound like Beavis and Butt-Head. Capable only of a strange kind of laughter. Hehehehehehehehe. As the rest of the world sleeps, this is me. Robotic zombie laughter, fetal position, ablaze.

It takes momentous willpower to drag myself to the bottle of whisky we have in the room. And all of my remaining energy to connect bottle to mouth. I sip it. Incipient.

I cannot stomach any more little sips.

My mind is on a rampage.

I wonder briefly about medical attention. Medical attention seems impossible. Also, expensive. A great regret of my life is to not have bathed before this overdose. And to not have sent an email to my mother.

I crawl to go be inside the closet. Hello darkness, my old friend. Here I am. All alone. About to die.

The shame itself of what I've been reduced to feels like a miscarriage of my soul.

June 4, 2011

Eventually, Cole threw all the bedding and towels from the room into the hallway for the laundry service to remove. Evidence I don't wish to hold onto. I wish he could have taken me out of the fire escape too. Left me beside the trash bin with the discarded refuse. Housekeeping can remake a bed and replenish towels. Housekeeping cannot rectify the aftermath of inhaling synthetic cathinones.

The ability to move eventually came back. Followed hours later by the ability to speak. I've gone through normative things: washing and eating some food. But inside, my mind is still smouldering. The scattered embers glow to illuminate swarming thoughts. My ditching of Barby, wondering how I'm going to explain myself to my grandmother, the various men I've been seeing recently, and all the different cities I have been flying between. Around a mountain of ash and burnt rubble, I can no longer run.

In this life I have twenty-seven years.

Exhausted, by afternoon, I'm on the floor by some lockers at Gate 10 C, LAX. I'm lying on the floor and breathing as deeply as I know how. In *Shavasana*. Corpse pose. Proper sleep still has not come to me. It's been about thirty-nine hours now. An hour ago I had to look a few people in the eye and search. For some mercy.

I had to ask the man standing behind me at the check-in counter if he could pay for my luggage. Plane tickets that exclude luggage don't make sense. Right now, everything is senseless. But with my bags checked and a boarding pass inside a handbag that's being used as a pillow, I can lie down and close my eyes.

A disturbing image haunts me. Thankfully, without review, in two quick clicks the traumatic footage on Cole's camcorder was erased. The same can't be said of the mental stills. These prove more permanent.

Breathe in. Breathe out.

I open my eyes.

Party On Darth. This is printed on the black T-shirt serving as a blanket. A shirt that used to belong to Cole.

On seeing a man dressed as Darth Vader standing beside us on Sunset Boulevard, he refused to continue wearing the shirt. I found the Darth plus Darth combination hilarious. Cole didn't. He bought a new shirt and gave me the old one.

For a relationship to endure, two people should find the same things funny. But the likelihood of compatibility with Cole is not worrisome. In fact, we will never see each other again.

Cole is boarding his own flight later today. Back to Afghanistan. The place he currently calls home.

Without emotion, his former T-shirt covers me. It smells like cologne, which baits some kind of romantic sentiment. Even though romance is far from the reality of being hurt. Physically. Mentally. I hurt. I try to think about nothing. The smell of cologne is a minor pleasantry.

I tell myself that I am in the right place and take a few more moments to look inwards. I try to let go.

Letting go now, I become an island. Alone still. But impenetrable. At sea.

Palming some Afghani dollars, these thoughts drift through my mind. With current inflation they're worth nothing, and with the current world view on Afghanistan they're not the best thing to be grasping onto in an American airport. Later, they will be moved onto a sterling silver platter beside my bed at my grandmother's house, amongst other lucky talismans. Various gems and vials and stones and feathers. A little interior decorating. Then I will move on and throw them away. Just as I will delete contact with the people who have seen me hit rock bottom. Finally.

Rock bottom is a place I have needed to end up at. It's certainly taken a while to arrive here. I am here now and it feels like a critical blessing.

By narrowly avoiding death, I am somehow alive. They say that Humpty Dumpty couldn't be put back together again. But this cannot be true. Addiction recovery often starts after a great fall.

I'm taking three flights with longish layovers to get home. I want my thoughts to turn off. I want to be in good shape and long-time sober. Not recovering from random narcotics or random guys. I want to sleep.

Through the skylight above, the sun warms my body and I float. At this exact moment I realize that the universe has been testing me, teaching me, and throwing every barrier in my way.

I continue to smile, faintly. Life has hurdles. Sometimes we trip. Sometimes we allow them to become permanent barriers. Some people are born jumpers. Some people practise and become agile, airborne. So I'm a runner after all. And can jump. And fell. Now I'm tired.

So I sleep. A deep and delicious sleep.

2

<del>||||</del> <del>||||</del> <del>||||</del> <del>||||</del> <del>||||</del> ||

"Discomfort should not be confused with pain."

June 5, 2011

Back at my make-shift room in the basement of my grandparent's house, no one is asking me any more questions and no one is making me feel worse than I already do. I nearly got arrested arriving home. Turns out that when I went missing from Vegas my mother filed a missing person's report. I'm furious with her. And confess nothing.

My grandma seems to understand that the most recent disappearing act is because I have no cell phone. Mobile phoneless herself, she knows there is freedom in disconnection. Even though she can sense there is more to my story, she respects me enough not to pry. I do not broadcast having arrived to an all-time low. The exact position I need to be in.

A baby bird in a nest. Fragile but gingerly optimistic.

Later, in a chair on the porch, I think about how to be a better granddaughter. This is a new role for me and impossible to fail at. Family tends to unconditionally love family.

From the array of flowers in full bloom in the garden, something echoes towards me. It floats off the notes of chirping birds and off the leaves rustling on the large oak tree. This sound is important. That I deserve to be happy. Above all, this is what everyone wants.

It's time to finally make lasting changes.

June 6, 2011

My plan remains simple. Twofold. I will learn French. And become asexual. For real this time.

To my right, a glass of juice and a chive plant. Behind me, the dogs mull aimlessly about the porch. To my left, a rock garden meticulously adorned with a multitude of tiny blossoms. I'm lying on a poncho-cum-blanket underneath the brilliant sun.

So far I have quit everything cold turkey. Continuation will require solitude. If discipline was a martial art, the black belt would be how to not let one glass be the landslide bringing me down. To that place of making a subsequent bad decision. Today, I feel perfectly fine. The binge-and-quit method seems to have allowed the inside of my body to start to cleanse. I want nothing more than to speed this up, so I went to a colonics clinic. The hydrotherapist performed the treatment and told me to chew more slowly. This is her explanation for my intestinal maladies. Grandma has the same council. My intestines, it seems, will be the last to heal. I don't elaborate to any of these specialists why my digestive tract is in disarray. Overconsumption of alcohol, feeling anxious and compulsive, and forcing myself to throw up are intertwined in a plait that is worn like a necklace without a clasp. Each time I fail to address these issues this accessory tightens. Quitting food is obviously not an option, but from this day onward I will unravel a strand. I will stop the emotional eating. I don't need to throw up. I imagine myself pulling apart the plait. The necklace breaks and three filaments fall to the floor.

June 7, 2011

Learning to speak French here is hindered by the fact that everyone also speaks perfect English. If one struggles to find words in one language, whomever they are in conversation with will just switch. Montrealers don't even realise that they do this. Perfect bi-lingualism.

June 8, 2011

Through a stroke of luck, and commenting *au française* to a Miami hotel's Facebook post, a Parisian man has befriended me online and offered me his vacant second bedroom in Paris, France, as the home base for a more authentic French immersion experience. It's at a financially affordable price: *au gratis*.

My grandma agrees that Paris is perfect. Cliché, maybe. But perfect.

Whether my past or my bad habits will come abroad this time, I don't know. Again, time will determine.

July 10, 2011

I walk to the Lachine Canal in the rain and pause to look out across the water. Standing in Mountain pose, I am tall and decide to welcome whatever wants to coexist. Holding my limbs, toes together and heels slightly apart, palms flipped forward, against the grey sky, extraneous past emotion doesn't veil my face. Naked to the elements, my forehead does what it wants to do. Scrunches. The past won't call the shots or bully me. It will just be given its own freedom. Then drift away.

*

August 10, 2011

Thankfully, France so far seems more interested in showcasing an assortment of cheese than in anything unpleasant. My English here is skill enough to find work. Bartending. Working at tradeshows. Etcetera. This doesn't feel exactly like a move forward, but I have to focus on the original plan.

Language improvement.
Behavioural modification.
Emotional stability.

August 22, 2011

My new roommate asks me how I'm doing so far and whether I foresee falling in love with anyone in the City of Lights. It's too soon for me to translate what I feel: a convergence of longing and hope and happiness and sadness. A full spectrum of potential emotions. Paris, it seems, is going to be a place to wait. I try to explain the second part of my plan. The asexuality. How I am someone who needs to stop using sex to ground my energy. Or, to get high off of.

So I will attend language class, work poorly-paying jobs, and wait. In the interim, I focus too on enjoying the local cuisine. It's delicious. All of it.

October 15, 2011

I cannot remember my life without the Seine, the Louvre, the Sacré-Cœur and Notre-Dame, la tour Eiffel, some Arches (one Grand and another Triumphant), the Opera, the Sorbonne, and endless cafés and manicured gardens as backdrop.

I take things in passively. Most of the time I am not aware of my precise location. Often phoneless and always without a watch or an agenda, in aimless promenade is when Paris is her best.

October 17, 2011

I have begun to investigate the local Yoga scene. Here right now seems to be a person in perpetual sunshine. On time for her engagements and living a life without hangovers or men. Except for the roommate. Though he is legitimately nice, he's also legitimately lonely. I can probably only be a guest here as long as I also agree to live rent-free in his heart. Someone to offset despondency. He had hoped we could be more than friends. Free housing or not, he reminds me a lot of my mother. Which I have told him. To make it very clear that we can be there for one another intellectually and spiritually. But purely platonically.

French cuisine alone is a great testing ground for my developing moderation. It is precise. It is held in high esteem. Simultaneously, wine flows more freely than water. Total abstinence is slightly insulting to what's on offer. So the name of the game is socially-refined indulgence. I have been described recently as a *bon vivant*. Refined in taste. But this has not been achieved without wobbles. Yesterday, I consumed an entire box of St Michel galettes au bon beurre. Afterwards, I felt disgusted. But then I waited. And did nothing, aside from forgive myself.

My future self will not devour an entire box of biscuits. She will acknowledge responsibility for what she puts into her body. Something slightly unhealthy, like processed sugar, will have its time and place if enjoyed in moderation. Give yourself what you need. But whatever you put inside, take responsibility for it. This is what I think, and it seems to be working.

As I lie down to sleep, my palms rest gently on my stomach, where they feel self-confidence, willpower, and intuition. Whether these things exist beneath a layer of fat or rock-solid abdominals also depends on what you put into the body.

November 1, 2011

In Paris, my mind wanders at liberty. Venturing less and less far. Inviting the mind to the permanence of stillness requires promise of a new room in which to live. Renovating my interior, an ongoing project.

I have already transferred into a more advanced French class.

This small milestone is a big reward.

In Yoga, with each Sun Salutation the uncertainty flows out of my body. The current Mantra is that I Am Strong. For all the times I've been scared, unsure, or quit. More than just salute the sun, I salute to vanquish all internal pollution.

November 8, 2011

Out and about, I have met some wonderful people who seem quintessentially Parisian. One is a model who invites me to hang out in chic lounges where we sit around tables with other model types. She is hard working, stylish, and undeniably sexy at all times. Another couple are culture snobs. Well-read, multilingual, gastronomic. I've become acquainted with art experts. Someone who rides an American motorcycle. An actor. I have met people who know everything about colonialism, others about outer space. I have dined at a former aristocrat's winter home turned library, art gallery, and restaurant. I've been invited into cute little flats with rooftop or courtyard views for French cocktail hour: *apéro*. I've been taken out to see things. Pop-up boutiques. Galleries. Vernissages. Local parks. Forests just outside the city. Country homes. Etcetera.

People here are friendly and inviting. The ambiance, so beautiful, often leaves me speechless. I am emerging *Mademoiselle Populaire en Paris*.

November 15, 2011

Travis recently emailed to confirm that Paris with a lover is incomparably romantic. Even as an asexual, I'm not impervious to this experience. In fact, I just said some big words. Three big words. I. Love. You. To myself. Doing this wasn't difficult. The exact opposite. It feels effortless.

December 3, 2011

French debate is different. Any topic seems permissible. From how things ought to be, to racially-based discrimination, to politics, to artistic merit. Nothing is off limits. Over 2008 Châteauneuf-du-Pape Rouge and a mature comté, I try to explain a little about who I am. And also, how I am in no way romantically linked to my roommate. I am met by a table of skeptics. Refined in palette, skeptical in presumption. They expect me to be guilty of some sort of catfishing. However, I maintain that I have never misled anyone with a false identity or broken promise. This may be the oldest form of angling: to simply use bait. What's being offered at the end of my line? Simply, friendship.

I struggle to translate this analogy and sense my living arrangement will not be so for much longer.

*

December 10, 2011

On a small hand-woven rug placed by the side of my bed, I stretch to close the door and begin a true Yin practice. Holding seated postures. Like Pigeon. And waiting.

The minutes are challenging. Even more than the morning news showing raw footage of a senseless street-style execution in Nigeria. The carnage is agitating. So is holding these poses for five to ten minutes. Flipping the channels, I found an especially gruesome investigative report on a synthetic opiate chemical drug, krokodil, alleged to be sweeping parts of Russia. Users become green, gangrenous, scaly, and lose chunks of rotten flesh. Death from the inside.

Holding postures for a long time is not painful. It is an observation. Yes there is pain in the world. Pain is real.

258

Discomfort should not be confused with pain. This is Yin and it's slowly arriving.

December 11, 2011

I like to venture to the grocery store or to my adopted sanctuary, Île Saint-Germain, the park next door. Underneath ancient trees, I rest. A sick mind, it seems, is just in the mind.

At this time of year the park is host to a sea of orange fallen leaves, families, and the Pony Club. Miniature horses being ridden by miniature humans. This scenery eventually breaks something inside me. Every part of myself lies in the grass, looking up to the sky. We are embedded in the universe. And miniscule.

Kahlil Gibran once said rest in reason, move in passion. Too many people rest depressed and move manic. Will my emotions permanently stabilize? My friend said to me the other day that happy and sad are a thin line. And so, life is sometimes sad. It is allowed to be that way because it includes things like rape, and torture, and death. We can accept those things because they are real. And also sad.

But the existence of sadness doesn't outweigh the existence of happiness. Sadness and happiness, I am beginning to learn, are attached. Nestled in the grass, I feel of a healthy mind and take a nap.

I dream that in addition to pain, and happiness, there is beauty. Like these city parks. The perfect life recipe, is to experience a bouquet of emotion. This is a perfect cycle, just like how the moon waxes and wanes. The continual dance between hopeless and hopeful is ever shifting and ever present.

December 12, 2011

The Yoga in France, compared to other places I've been, is less of a parade. Tucked inside a courtyard, if I didn't know to come to this studio on the instruction of a friend, I wouldn't see it. Like many things tucked away in courtyards, secret Yoga studios exist. Hidden from the street, in this room there's nothing fancy. The students aren't wearing the newest over-priced mirco-shorts, drinking import fusion tea elixir, or jumping into handstands. Not yet anyway. Corporate Yoga will probably go on. I just don't see it right now.

During practice, the discomfort deep beneath my shoulder blades, that was once called scar tissue, finally leaves me. During a standing forward bend, arms extended overhead, fingers clasped together in *mudra*. Something clicks and the pain releases. It's gone. Years of pain, lifted.

There will always be days where every moment feels like too much effort. Like a sweater slowly unravelling. One run away thread, which holds together the entire garment, goes awry. Even in the sunshine. Even with cocktails. Cappuccinos. Treats. Compliments. A designer jacket. Fresh blossoming flowers. Art in the streets. Church bells. Chocolate. And messages from beloved friends. All I can feel some days is this thread. Unravelling.

But mostly there are other days. Where everything fits. Where everything flows.

I try to remember these better days. Happy memories are better transportation than bad memories. I'm not sure I'm trying to get away, anyway. Actually, stillness arrives.

Then, a sensation of gliding.

I thought this feeling was forever lost in my youth. It's back. I'm gliding. Weightless and without friction. In slow motion, I stop to look around. At the park on the outskirts of Paris, each individual blade of grass sways with the slightest of motion. Sun shimmers off these blades. In this grass, sadness and happiness become the same thing. The ground and the sky converge and

turn into one. Situational satisfaction becomes possible for an
eternity.

December 19, 2012

On a hard wooden floor, nestled on a sheep skin, I meditate and
embrace the silence. In the distance, beyond the patio and the
Seine, a star shines through tree branches. In a glimmer of light,
a whisper tells me how to be comfortable in my own skin.

I read once that that the most beautiful people are those
who have known defeat, known suffering, known struggle,
known loss, and have found their way out. These people have
an appreciation, sensitivity, and understanding of life that fills
them with compassion, gentleness, and deep, loving concern.

I

卌 卌 卌 卌 卌 |||

"Where the mind forgets, the body remembers."

January 5, 2012

Because they love me, my parents enrolled me in a registered Yoga teacher training program. It happens to be in Vancouver. This city is the past and this course, the future. My memories of events are changing even more.

Evidentially, the human being has two containers of memory. The mind as well as the body. To alter the mind and adapt how we think, remember, and interpret, we must alter the body. This is because where the mind forgets, the body remembers. Yoga as an outlet can re-sculpt muscle memory. As long as you are alive you will go through things and you will remember them at some level. But you will not suffer.

This is what Yoga offers. Life is not suffering.

January 7, 2012

In lecture today the teacher reiterates that scars and emotional turmoil are not mutually exclusive. We tend to think of scars as the physical and emotions as the mental, but they are related. They are one and the same.

A nervous mind causes tension and stiffness. Yoga, the ancient form of stillness, trains the opposite. Quantity stops and quality prevails. Around me our exhalations become powerful, warm, and vibrant. Like garlands of dewy petals extending from the crown.

January 10, 2012

Life at a Yoga college is Yogafied. Walking is Yoga. Using the toilet is Yoga. Existence is Yoga.

All of it makes me want to cleanse. To rid myself of useless internal waste.

January 12, 2012

A lot of things are coming up. The process is overwhelming. Thankfully, my teacher and the other students offer support. Like pillars.

Sipping fragrant loose-leaf jasmine tea, the woman I have been listening to endlessly sits in front of us. She is regal and draped in velvet. Reassuringly, she agrees that Yoga is Life. Then she stops to laugh. Because everything is also nothing. And this is quite hilarious.

The abstract nature of this syllabus doesn't confound me. Most of it I inherently understand. Things that marijuana and philosophy taught along the way. But what about chasing other things? My luxuries habits for instance. It seems years of learning to think about wanting and needing create mental and even physical holding patterns. Years of Yoga can rearrange these thought processes. And reality changes.

Being a prisoner to any type of persistent thought is suffering. The philosophy of Yoga says that most people's minds are cluttered with a combination of poisonous thoughts.

January 15, 2012

As the days go by, I feel less and less poisoned. As homework

I read about the three root poisons: greed, hate, and delusion. The opposites show virtuous characteristics: generosity, loving-kindness, and wisdom. The prevailing notion is that by detaching from desire, accepting the un-pleasurable, and reconstructing the I / me dialogue, something magical will happen.

According to my notes, by letting go of how we come to define ourselves in the world, it is possible to open a gate. Not to some other room, but to an intangible opening to explore and be curious in. Right now. All of this proves that we are not who we think we are. Anything is possible.

Transformation itself is not a surprise. It's the outcome. Don't be surprised if balanced *prana* changes your demeanour. Someone once attached to her headphones will no longer blast music into her ears. She will enjoy listening to whatever sounds happen to be going on around her.

At Yoga college we're not instructed to go on a special Yoga diet. I've just been inspired to experiment with consumption of raw vegan food, zero coffee and no alcohol. Let's see how it suits me.

We have been discussing separating from the I-ness of life, thoughts, and emotions. The result is an existence of nearly ultimate presence where we can truly be in the moment. Here, it becomes possible to make ultimate decisions.

January 16, 2012

More and more emotions are rapidly coming up. I dream of abandonment. Of all the things from my past that, despite being unhealthy and harmful, I clung to. I wake up more than crying. Sobbing. I also wake up to a personal celebration. I'm not scared of this pattern continuing.

The room we create by opening up to silence allows for vital life force from the universe to animate the body, feed the soul, and lift the mind. I keep saying it but it's worth repeating. It took years of preparing for something incredible. Finally, it's happening.

January 18, 2012

In the classroom I'm surrounded by an array of students. Bodybuilders. Naturopaths. Those seeking a career-change. Even those simply curious for no apparent reason. Some of the students have been drinking urine. Others will go on to change their names in spiritual transformation or live in total harmony with the environment. Some of us, myself included, have a way to go to rest in a good place. Not that anyone would judge this. In fact, no one here passes judgement at all. Amongst Yogis, you are likely to be very safe.

It is helpful to be amongst these people.

January 27, 2012

I feel like the person I want to be. Balanced. Whether this has all been training, progress, or a return does not matter.

A point arrives where you're not just aware of your own energy and the energy in others, but where you master the capacity to rebuild and retain energy. This, an aspect of *tantra*. To rebuild. To preserve. The amount of work you have to do depends on the lives you have led and are leading, past and present. Conveniently, I'm not afraid of hard work.

At the Yoga graduation ceremony we chant four simple words. *Om Mani Padme Hum*. Meaning, you are the jewel in the centre of the lotus. This chant has the power to affect the children of our great grandchildren. A powerful concept.

In each of our hands is a certificate that designates us as Yoga Teacher. Not in hand, without designation, an ability to be present. Something that starts in fleeting moments. Like being beside someone and actually seeing them. Or being in conversation and actually listening.

Though officially certified, I have been told that I need more grounding. This advice doesn't come as a shock. But it will be a difficult feat for someone whose body is due on yet another airplane.

It's off towards the unknown once more.

*

February 25, 2012

One of the students at Yoga school introduced me to her friend. He has invited me on an adventure. It's a long way to go. By now extreme distance is not daunting.

Through the glass wall at an airport Starbucks coffee shop, I look at the horizon. At the sun rise over Kuala Lumpur, Malaysia. I've flown here overnight.

As I sip water in the balmy airport, the blanket of darkness retreats. A process that takes approximately half an hour. Just about the amount of time you should dedicate to waking the body each morning. Introducing it to the day ahead. It's an introduction. It needs time. Time to become acquainted. Even at the first light of dawn, this city is alive. Brilliant and animating.

I am going onward to Koh Samui, an island in the Gulf of Thailand. Here because it is life that hurts us. That damages us. But it is also life that heals us.

The destination, a natural health resort.

Greeting me at the airport is a professional gambler, ticket scalper, and hustler. He is a friend of my new Yoga sister and has been coming to Thailand for years. The party circuit eventually led him to the detox circuit. Both of which are well established here.

At the detox spa my observation is that both a lot and nothing go on. I decide to wander down to the beach and watch people. The plan here is to fast. To slow down and cleanse. I sense that when your body doesn't have to expend energy on digesting, its awareness of everything else heightens. I welcome this sensitivity.

February 28, 2012

The faster's diet is to eat nothing. The official program couples drinking a soup of bentonite clay and psyllium husk with undergoing twice-daily enemas. These serve to flush unhealthy bacteria and toxins from the body.

Unsurprisingly, the intensive cleansing is intensive. Without getting too graphic, enemas involve inserting a small tube into the anus to siphon a mixture of filtered water and coffee into the colon. You can lie on your side and hold the fluid in, or you can practise simple inversions. Self-massage of the stomach helps to facilitate the intestinal cleaning.

Then you release the fluid. And the old, the wasted, and the toxic are flushed away.

March 1, 2012

To benefit from energetic healing, I am participating in a reiki session.

I lie atop a thatched mattress arranged on the tile floor of an outdoor terrace. The tree canopy whistles above. Part of a larger jungle fortress. The breeze beyond whispers a background song.

The healer places his hands above my body. Sometimes pressing lightly and sometimes not. We go deep. I envision colours, patterns, images, and emotions. My ultimate music video.

The mental scenery changes.

I see myself being born and observing the world for the first time. I see myself being sexually violated. I see descriptionless faces and fire. Some of these faces burn. Others extinguish. Only ambers remain.

Then, I float underwater. In caves. I wonder what evils or joys exist around each rocky barrier. I can feel wind and rain and wetness and cold. I feel the ocean. The magnificent power and unbridled force of the water. By my heart, I am surprised. At how much healing remains. By my navel, so many old emotions. Things I have pushed far down, compacted into the area beneath my belly button.

My heart couldn't handle it all.

Then, the treatment stops.

I slowly open my eyes and sit up, cross-legged. I am beside the therapist, reset to not knowing anything. Never all-knowing, always growing. Sensations like this are cyclical in the Yoga path.

March 5, 2012

One should expect to experience some degree of emotional turbulence while cleansing. Emotions are an acute effect of toxins being leaked from the body. In my case, the things that continue to come out of my ass look like pure evil. Otherworldly. Similar to garbage that has been breaking down in the ocean for decades. Soupy, chemical, nasty. Nothing I want to associate with that which ought to be on the inside.

March 7, 2012

At the local Yoga studio we start with a series of standing postures. Everything seems routine. Reaching our hands towards the ceiling, we begin to tilt our bodies to the side into Half Moon pose. Each individual strand of hair brushes delicately past my face, then, not so delicately, I crash down.

My head is buzzing like a thousand bees on the brain. The dim room is spotty and a bump is growing where my head hit the floor below.

The teacher is crouching over me.

Without food, it's possible to feel energised from the ocean, the moon, and local friends. Without food, one should not attempt a ninety-minute-long Yoga class. This is called overexertion.

It turns out that during a fast many people become off balance. It turns out that I am no different to many people.

I let myself be pulled to the tide of the ocean. Obtain a front-row seat to its ebb and flow. In and out. Just like my breath.

As I turn to look behind me, the trees lining the beach all move in unison. Like an extension of my lungs. The rhythm of the universe. They grow on an inhalation and contract on an exhalation. On closer inspection, I can see individual leaves on individual trees. These leaves are also moving. They jump out, bright green, as the sole interruption to the total nothingness. The total silence that I revel in.

March 9, 2012

It seems that my tolerance for the heat is dwindling, a revived tan aside. Can too much time beside the ocean become overindulgent? I no longer feel like only my head's off the ground. Now, the entire body. Lifts away.

Some birds are migratory. They live in one location during the winter and another during the summer. But to be a bird in flight does not mean to soar above the clouds forever.

At some point we all need to feel grounded. To feel at home.

O

𝍸 𝍸 𝍸 𝍸 𝍸 𝍷𝍷𝍷𝍷

"To live is to be awakened."

August 1, 2012

On the level of Astrology, once we let go, we can become less prone to the suggestions of a past. By creating room, anything can happen.

Chapters of our life are all just a cycle. They come and go. Like sunlight and darkness. Life and death. Cellular division. Your personal chapters may seem haphazard, but they are not. Just as there are eight phases of the moon, twenty-four hours in a day, and 365 days in a year. Life's chapters are governed by strong external forces in dance with internal forces. Universal. Spiritual. Magical.

Here I am at the crux of my first Saturn Return, one of the many things continuously coming full circle. It's both amazing and challenging. Instead of trying to dissect the meaning of absolutely everything, I'm learning to allow myself to be washed over. To surrender. To receive.

You can view your successes or problems under a microscope, or just let them be.

It's obvious that addiction is not balance. Less obvious, addiction is neither a behaviour nor a substance. Bold letters scrawled across a whiteboard in my dream told me that.

Addiction is a place.

By diverting energy away from what creates addictions, away from those places, addiction no longer exists. The central nervous system no longer prefers to exist on overdrive or deadly sedation. We're too often taught that to live is to be wired in synaptic symphony. Fight or flight, then unconscious and asleep. Not true.

To live is to be awakened.

The amount of energy it takes to repair the type of damage caused by creation without pause, reckless partying, excessive drinking, nymphomania, or gluttony is more than we can replenish just in sleep.

We must look inwards.

My past vices do not need to be brutally murdered. I have been far too hard on myself. It seems instead that they can rest eternally. They can sit in a nice chair that floats in a pool. A fortress surrounded by a moat. A jewel in the centre of a lotus.

Like this, you can channel internal light. Similar to how children direct sunbeams through a magnifying glass to burn paper.

Your fires shall become a pilot light.

A source.

If you loved this book, please leave a review,
tell a friend, and spread the word.